Electricity Slides

John Brady McDonald

Published by
BookLand Press Inc.
15 Allstate Parkway
Suite 600
Markham, Ontario L3R 5B4
www.booklandpress.com

Printed in Canada

Front cover image by Sebdeck

Library and Archives Canada Cataloguing in Publication

Title: Electricity slides / John Brady McDonald.
Names: McDonald, John Brady, 1981- author.
Description: Series statement: Modern Indigenous voices.
Identifiers: Canadiana (print) 20210156945 | Canadiana (ebook) 20210156961 | ISBN 9781772311495 (softcover) | ISBN 9781772311501 (EPUB)
Classification: LCC PS8625.D646 E44 2021 | DDC C811/.6—dc23

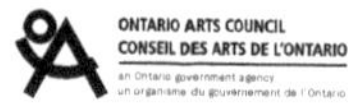

We acknowledge the support of the Government of Canada through the Canada Book Fund and the support of the Ontario Arts Council, an agency of the Government of Ontario. We also acknowledge the support of the Canada Council for the Arts.

This book is dedicated to
the Dadaists and the Iconoclasts

PROLOGUE

"Where is your Commander?"
"He is gone, sir, and we don't know where he is."
"How many are left down there, son?"
"There is no one left down there, sir."
"Did they run away from the field, too?"
"No one is running away down there, sir. The Dead don't run."

CHAPTER I

I sat deep within the supple red leather of the oversized armchair; my thin frame nearly undetectable when looked at from the side. I wore a black pair of slacks and a white dress shirt, buttoned almost to my neck, with no tie. Around me were piled mounds and mounds of books; hardcover tomes mingled with paperbacks and scrapbooks. Hundreds of them occupied the massive room that was the warehouse.

The chair was located in the corner of the cavernous open area, underneath the dead tubes of the fluorescent lights that hung from the rafters at awkward angles. The chair faced the enormous corrugated steel loading bay door that faced east, though the chair was several metres away from it.

I inhaled deeply, relishing the dank smell of my surroundings. The dust and mildew of the building and its contents mingled with the stench of the garbage that lay piled in what was once the foreman's office.

To the side of the chair stood a gaudy swag lamp, its green plastic shade glowing defiantly in the face of the burnt-out lights above. A small oak table stood beside the lamp, and upon it stood an ink well and a feather quill pen, as well as other knick-knacks.

I stood from the chair and stretched languidly. The night had been long and drawn out, and the activities in which I had been engaged had been exhausting.

I wallowed in the self-pity of wasted talent and wasted time. I was playing air guitar to the masses and not asking why. Rooms filled with apathetic energies, draining everything from everyone. There was no real joy, only superficial sorrow.

I had sought it out and lost it. Squandered genius behind bloated excess. I watched the crowds with too much money, but not enough food, and yet they would consume, consume, in a capitalistic orgy of intake of everything their plastic cards and rectangles of paper could get them. They would feast and eat and feast and shit. Throw it up and start again. The men on the line did the same thing, day after day, only what they consumed was dirt, a few miles of dirt each day, paying for it with chunks of metal hurled at great speed.

Thus, began my disdain for propaganda. I had no time for empty bliss. I sought out the mysteries of the cube, and all I found was burning and dying.

I soon discovered that the core of it all is the need. I was punished for withholding the poison. I would bargain with myself, "Please, spare me the ignorance of materialistic youth." Yet, all I found was blood in my stomach, blood in my eyes, hiding from the voices, whispering to me, coming to get me, convincing myself that they're outside the door. Death was in my stomach. Death was in my eyes, soaking my conscience.

So, I found myself in an abandoned place, a forgotten place. Forgotten so much so that they never even disconnected the electricity to it.

I surrounded myself with what I needed at that time. The shelves dipped with the weight.

I had read every book upon them. They were heavy with the weight of knowledge. That much weight can kill a man if not taken carefully.

At first, I sat and gazed upon the rows of them; each one a story told and retold. I would take one from the strip and hold it in my hands. I learned all over again that it was alive once, and that some poor bastard sat there and plucked those words out of the sky and put them in that order, and that it was now my duty to take it in, follow the lines, make it live again. I had to learn to be okay with the knowledge that to be a romantic is to die alone, to be a poet is to starve, to be an artist is martyrdom, that creativity is a sadistic bastard and that, to be these things meant to be deprived of rest and peace.

I walked to a stack of books nearly seven feet tall. I looked at the stack from several different angles, circling the pillar of books. I drew my finger slowly down the spines of the books as one would draw their finger down the keys of a piano. My finger stopped when I found the one I was looking for, halfway between the floor and the top.

I studied the stack, attempting to find a way of removing it from the stack without upsetting the pile. In the end, I simply placed my hand upon the stack and pushed it over.

The books showered down upon the floor, the cacophony of dull thuds and the sharp smacks of hardcover books solidly hitting bare concrete echoed through the warehouse. A mushroom cloud of dust wafted through the air as I bent down to retrieve the book I wanted.

Walking back to the chair, I wiped the dust off the front of the book, a newer paperback. It was black, with red, Germanic writing proclaiming the title, "Dracula," and its author, Bram Stoker.

I inserted my thumbnail randomly into the book, and opened it to that spot. My hazel eyes began to gaze upon the words, and I read aloud some of the passages.

"...or it may sound the death knell of the Un-dead who walk the earth." My voice echoed throughout the dead building. I smirked as I closed the covers of the book and gazed upon the cover.

"Eastern European legends corrupted through Victorian eyes," I said. I threw the book into the air in an arc, as if I was tossing a Frisbee to a dog. The book left the light of the lamp and landed somewhere in the darkness with a resounding smack.

I knew what I needed to best get the results from my work. I set the scene and awaited the players. The chaos and clutter of the books and papers had to be perfect in my eyes for success.

I looked to the books at my feet. With the toe of my left shoe, I lightly opened the cover of a leather-bound book of some large size, much like a ledger. Inside, the pages were a soft beige colour, and were as blank and bare as the soul of an infant.

I picked up the book, and, turning on my heel, headed back for the arm chair.

I sank heavily into the soft leather, and reaching for the bottle of ink to my side, I opened the ledger book to the first page.

I picked up the closed jar of black India ink. I shook it back and forth for a few moments, and then carefully unscrewed the lid. The black ink in the bottle reflected the light above only slightly. I balanced the jar carefully upon my knee, and, picking up the feather quill pen, I dipped the quill into the ink.

A few droplets of ink flicked upon the leather of the chair. They rolled down the softened sides and disappeared between the cushion of the chair and my thigh.

"Shit," I said. I really didn't care, but it just seemed like the most logical response. I lowered the quill to the paper, and, with the experienced hand of one who had written for years with that style of pen, I deftly began to write.

"I have always found it funny, how 'they' try to capture what it is truly like. Oh well, what can one expect from those whose life span comes to a short and abrupt end; a being that sees the passing of seven or eight decades between their birth and death as a 'long life'."

I stopped and dipped the pen into the ink once more. I continued.

"Birth and death. Living and dying. I too once had the same visions, once upon a time." I stopped. I looked at those last four words, and, shaking my head, moved to cross them out. I stopped short, however, and left them alone. I reached into my pocket. It was still in there, or they were, to be correct. I pulled one out and stared at it for a moment, then put it back. Now was not the time. Not yet. I had to get this down first. I continued to write. "'Once Upon a Time.' Rather a clichéd start to this tale, is it not? 'Once Upon a Time.' Men have made fortunes from starting their stories that way. Well, I guess it's as good a way to start a story as any, the final act. Once Upon a time...."

The Scene: A small restaurant lost in the middle of nowhere.

I had been sitting alone in a booth. I was sipping bad coffee and writing bad prose.

Her purple faux-fur coat first caught my eye. It glowed in the dawn's morning light. "Where the hell have you been?" she asked me.

I looked up and smiled. "I'm here, and that's good enough."

Some people just can't take a hint when you're trying to be an asshole.

She sat down without asking if she could. She asked me what I was writing.

"I'm writing new lines for highway signs," I said without looking up.

She giggled and said, "Sounds fun. What does it say?"

She was always a crazy girl. She'd sit at a table and drink coffee creamers. She was like a bad cold that you just can't shake, no matter how many pills you take, and out of all of the girls I told I loved, she was one of two that I regretted saying those words.

I pushed the notebook over to her. The paper read:

"Watch your step
We're really not sure what's in there
Here may be dragons
Or here may be ghosts."

She had the face of a mime. I waited for words of wisdom from her. She had the words of a mime, too.

I decided to look her in the eyes. It was always on a dare, a challenge to the mind, when you looked into those eyes. It was bad timing, a slip of the tongue. It paid the price of my admission.

"What is it you want, exactly?" I made the mistake of asking.

She sat back, her faux blonde hair falling over her eyes. "I want some fun."

A highway is an overrated experience. We passed a sign that read 'Respect and Honour our Majestic Roadways'. Not I. Someone else can respect. I will abuse it to excess.

I looked over at her, and at the speedometer. There was no real need to be going so fast, but the needle crept past 160.

"In a hurry?" I asked her.

She said nothing, but the ball of her foot pressed harder into the pedal.

I turned and stared out the window. Nothing was said between us and nothing was implied until she brought the car to a skidding halt.

Out the door and down the drive, she scraped her ratty high-top shoes down the way. As we walked down the gravel road, we could see the places where something had killed a bird. All was gone. Only feathers remained. I watched as the crows flocked to the place where they had dumped all the fur and the bones. They called for the others, their caws echoing through the still, bare trees. Soon, other crows would arrive to take ownership of the spoils.

"What do you think?" she asked.

I looked up to an old abandoned house in a forgotten bland part of the world. "I don't think," I replied.

She wanted to hold my hand as we stepped over the threshold. Her artificial nails matched my artificial affection and interest perfectly. I sighed quietly, not wanting to kick up the dust, both on the floor and in our minds.

She turned on her heel, and before I knew it, the cube was between my lips and onto my tongue. She stood smiling and I stood shocked.

It was too late to go back. My fate was sealed. The trip had begun. It was done so subtly, but soon I would be lost. We were inside the farmhouse when it kicked in. I couldn't see anything, but I could feel everything. My ears caught bits of Beethoven, and I could taste the last of the summer chokecherries. The smell of pure prairie age hit me.

She asked again, "Here we are. What do you think?"

If she knew what I truly thought, I knew I'd be walking home. "What's your plan?" I asked.

Her plastic nails pushed deep into my palms. "Let's set it on fire," she said out of the blue.

♦ ♦ ♦

The amount of damage that a single match can cause on a hot, dry summer's day, the speed at which the flames move, cascading waves of shimmering heat. You cannot outrun it. You can try, but you won't make it.

Smoke curled into the sky, black and grey against the blue. The smell of burning wood and oil carried on the wind. Behind the smoke, the sun hid. Below the sun the trees burn. Fire eats the forest whole, and the ashes rain down where water should fall, but such is the state of things today.

Multicoloured clouds of dust turned my sinuses into open sores. The pain of one thousand hammers beating upon my skull from the inside out. Enough to keep me awake at night.

"What the fuck did you do?" I gasped, staring over my shoulder through the window of the car.

She laughed a little girl laugh as an old song played on the radio.

The cube had been very small. "It's wearing off," I said. "Get me some more or get me home."

The accelerator touched the floor. The speedometer needle buried itself again deep in the dashboard. Gravel flew and spit into the ditch behind us.

Her hand disappeared deep into her pocket and once again, between my lips and on my tongue. Here we go again. My stomach churned with each rattling jolt. Keep it down, and keep it in. you need it all for the party to begin. My seatbelt began to feel like a lover's arms around my waist and across my chest. That seemed to be the way I liked it best.

"I need to get away from you," I finally screamed over the noise. "You're becoming a bad influence on me."

She chuckled as she passed me a bottle. "That's a load of shit," she said. "I'm just the person mommy warned you about."

I meant to speak after I took a drink, but wouldn't you know it, the words began to fade away. "What was in the water?" I finally gasped.

She smiled. "Only the tickets to the next ride,"

My lips went numb, and my legs gave way. I closed my eyes, but the images were too crazy. "Not cool," I blurted towards what I thought was her.

"Not yet," the voice came from the lights around me.

Lights of all kinds, all shapes. I'd rather curse the candle and lust for the darkness.

"Centre line!" she screamed at me, "the centre of the line!"

Fuck, what a scream.

"Sonny boy," he said with a sweep of his hand, "have I got a story for you."

I looked up. "Excuse me?"

He sat down next to me. "I said, if you want a story, I have one I can tell you."

"I didn't know I was looking for a story," I replied.

We were on a beach. The beach was all but deserted. Storm clouds had driven away the crowds, along with the sun and the warmth of the past week. It reminded me of those holiday photos that my grandmother had of her childhood in England; of toddlers in raincoats and hats standing on a black and white beach.

The man reached into his pocket and took out an old chunk of tissue. He unrolled it.

I stood up. "Keep it," I said. "I've got enough stories for a while."

His old man hand clutched at my sleeve. "Not like this one," he said. "This story is a sonofabitch, makes people crazy. Causes a man to cut his own dick off and flush it down the toilet. You'll want to hear it."

What can a soul do when given such a choice? I now needed to hear a tale that could cost me my cock. I sat down.

The tissue was old and yellow. The Skeleton key it held was older and darker. "This key," he said, "doesn't open shit."

"Fair enough," I said, and stood to leave again. And again, the old man hand clutched my sleeve.

"Here, take it." He said. And he plopped it into my hand. I held it and stared. "Now what?" I asked.

He pointed to the lake. "Throw it as far into the water as you can. Go on."

I stood and lobbed it into the air. It splashed a metre from shore. "And?" I asked.

He laughed and smiled. "Look at your hand," he said.

I looked down, and saw that they key was still there. When I looked up, he was running down the beach. "It's yours now, sonny! It's a magic talisman for the voodoo queen!"

It slipped into my pocket and stayed there the summer. When I meet the voodoo queen, though, she's taking it from me.

Strange times. The floodlights hurt my eyes at least a dozen times a day. Behind those ramparts, with the snipers, is where I should've stayed. I am in limbo, for this is all very new. I'm unsure of what is coming down. The bottle said "drink me" and the book said "read me". My mother told me always to obey.

There were so many questions I needed to ask. When did my hair turn grey? When did I lose my youth? Since when does this body belong to me?

My mind is somewhere else on this cold November evening. I am not here, but in Paris, sitting along the river. I had disembarked from the train, and the platform was bustling with people. I was smoking cigarettes and looking for the man who would find me. His speech was Anglophone. He said that he was with the French Resistance. He didn't believe me when I told him that we had won the war.

He stubbed his cigarette out on the back of my hand. "Bring the fight to Berlin," he hissed. "I'm here. I've always been here. Where else can I go?"

I spat into his eyes. "I remember the day you ceased being a man and became a fool, the day where your tragic life became a waste of talent. The day I wept for you, and moved on."

I stood and crossed the street. Up the stairs, third door to the left. Open this door, and turn on the light. This was an empty room; bare walls and bare floor. One lonely fly buzzed around the naked light bulb.

"Drink me," the bottle cried again. My feet were cold and my arms shivered, but I knew my Greek history. The gods will arrive.

A visit of sorts was planned. The table was set, of course, with my favourite things: paper and pens. I was planning on a long visit, late into the night, ready to forge ahead with plans and ideas. Spelling on the paper, writing on the wall, the mystic smashing of hammers upon the barriers where we were kept away from the noises at night, away from the gaze of the Machine.

It seemed put upon by the ghosts of those foolhardy and headstrong as they tried their very best to keep the masses in line with their doctrines.

I sat down and began to write. The words get harder to read the faster you write. Your hand drags through the ink, leaves black smudges on the page, and on the skin of your fingers. The pen exploded masturbatory, ink and seed splashed all over, but it was okay. Black mirrored shades hid my eyes. Avoid the desire to smash the bulb and slice the paper and cut your wrists and bleed everywhere.

She knew where she could find me, and she did find me, huddled like a Bedouin sheltered from the storm. I looked into her lying eyes to see what I could read.

The wind blew through the open window. The curtains fluttered to one side. That stack of papers on the table caught air and spread themselves upon the floor. She stood at the window, looking out. She looked to the sea, gazing for answers. "If the sea held answers, then all the Captains and Sailors would be leaders," she said.

"Your bullshitting sincerity is all in vain," I chuckled. "For all I have to do is step outside that door, and you will never see me again."

She pulled a long blade from her boot. "I tried to break it to you gently, but you wouldn't pay attention to me. I draw my sword as you draw your gaze away from this exchange? Are we to play doctor today?"

"I wouldn't pull on that chain, if I were you," I said. "You never know what kind of a dog is on the other end."

"Last night, I dreamt that they were taking the innocent away. Hundreds of them, in the old city buses of my youth." She trembled. "I screamed at them to stop, only to realize that I was one of the people they made shepherd them towards the parking lot."

"Sometimes you need to question why, and sometimes you need to do what you're told." I replied.

She slashed at me. "Who will let the people know? Who will assuage their fears? Are you willing to lie? Will you go on record? Will you bullshit all and say, 'relax, everything will be alright?' What good is pulling teeth when they only give you water?"

I stood and stared down at her. "I cannot ascertain your deductive reasoning." My stomach began to claw at me like a housecat trying to get in. My blood was emptying, but the diesel plant was still plugging away.

"Speaking of engines," I said as she thrust at me with the knife, "Has anyone ever told you that you sound like an old tractor when you cum? I wouldn't worry too much about it, though, Blondie. A little turpentine should clean out your combustion system, but I wouldn't hold your breath. There's only so much you can ask poison to do."

The door crumbled as I slammed it. With any luck, she was going to stay in there, absently slashing at her torso with that knife.

♦ ♦ ♦

They let us use the hall. We dimmed the house lights low. Murmurs in the crowd carried past the curtained stage. Even the stagehands could make out the words.

"We want the show," they chanted. "Give us the show!" They are no fools. They are here to be entertained, and who are we to deny them? Raise the curtain!

The wino at the end of the hall danced in time to the ticking of the pipes above his head. I shouted at him, and he smiled back. "You act like a crazy man, mister," he said through missing teeth. "You enjoy the attention that it brings, you pass the hat, and then you keep the change inside." He kicked off his shoes and threw them out the window. "Take all that money, and put a down payment on the dream. That's what you should have done, but you tripped the wire, and you set the whole world on fire. You stepped out of bounds and lost your right to it all!"

I turned to walk away, but he followed. "Your mouth says 'yes', but your eyes say 'fuck off'. I'd take the hint, if only you would throw out the bait, mister."

The stick in my hand is rough, and hitting the stone steps with it is making my fingers bleed. I'll pull the splinters out tomorrow. Head spinning, room swimming, ears are ringing, but it's my own doing.

The wino kicked my legs. "You hated them all for the colour of your skin and the roundness of their eyes, mister. That's not the way of a gentleman." He took my hand.

"I caught you in your lies, mister." He spat the combination of a lock he'd lost the week before.

The audience cheered.

I stepped over him and headed for the alley door. I needed to get to the dark place while nothing made sense.

Sewer rats and alley cats and three-legged dogs fought over scraps of flesh in the yard. The rain dropped down my neck. I still held the stick and I struck again; all my strength into a featherweight blow. I wanted to sit and watch the asphalt equinox, the sidewalk solstice of the alleyway. The seasons change little on the street. It's one less warm day, one more layer to throw over your shoulder.

It's clear to the street people that a poor man's soul is valuable indeed. So many seek it to fill their respective ethereal coffers. You can find the Cobblestone Christians standing there, hawking their wares. "Hey, buddy, trade your soul for a cup of coffee? Salvation with a sandwich?"

It climbed up into my head like a spider, and now I could see them all, this pantheon of religious pimps. The Dumpster Druids cast their circles with cinder blocks and the Black Leather Buddha with golden hair screaming into a payphone. A Blue Jean Jesus strung from a power pole, being pierced in the side by sanitation workers trying to pull him down. "Oh, Sweet Jesus! There he goes again!" They cried out, as the parasitic electrical conduits crackled to life. They began to vent out massive amounts of wasteful electronic and stereoscopic pollution, none of which was healthy or beneficial to the crowds, most of whom were registered voters who punctually filed their income taxes.

Meanwhile, the Apostle was sitting on a stoop waxing tales as the Electric Monk was lost somewhere in prayer beside him. "They shot the dead guru into the night sky," he said. "He had his ashes loaded and mingled with firework dust." He undulated his hands. "The other guru died an old man, still humping the dreams and memories of a heroin addiction from fifty years ago." He smiled. "It just goes to show you what happens when you make friends with a Hollywood movie star."

I sat down between the two of them. A bottle was passed to me in a brown paper bag. I brought it to my lips, but before I could drink, a filthy hand came between them, and I kissed the leathery dirty skin.

"Before you take communion with us, brother," the Apostle croaked, "You must share your words. Speak your truth, Youngblood. The truth shall set you free!"

I wished that I could have crawled into my skull so that I could solder the tethers back together enough to string some words together. It was a lot to ask to drink from a hobo's wine bottle.

My lips began to mumble something along the lines of, "and thus the gods of man commune but what of the Goddesses? All of them waiting for the tide to change. Hippies dance around the fire's light."

The two of them began to laugh the old hacking laugh of a homeless drunk. I soon joined in, though I knew that I was laughing at myself.

"You need this more than we do, Youngblood," the Apostle clapped me on the back and handed me back the bottle. He stood and shook his partner beside me. "Did you hear that? Those quatrains of prophesy from our boy here, the latter-day Nostradamus!" He laughed and spat on the ground. "You go on and try to sell that bullshit down over there." He pointed to the sandwich and coffee crowd. "Those are the bleak and broken ones, casting shade over the coming."

The Electric Monk coughed and grabbed hold of my left hand. He squeezed hard. "Half of what is yet to come has passed into what is now, and whatever is left is shuffled back into the deck of what could be."

I looked at the Apostle. "What does that mean?" I asked.

He smiled. "Who knows?" he said. "He's drunk."

I shakily stood up. I fell into the arms of the Apostle.

"Easy, Youngblood. If you want to change the path or change the way or divert the course, by all means, try your best, and do it well. Just remember that no words, no thoughts, and no peace can come to you while chasing after her."

I looked at him astonished. "How did you know about her?" I asked.

He smiled. "You think you're the first little boy who's forgotten to run away with the circus when it left town?"

I began to run down the sidewalk.

He stood there, as the three-legged dog gnawing the toes off his bare feet. "Obstruction is an ugly way to settle things, mister," he sang out. "Destruction breaks away the scene. Call upon a telephone somewhere in the distance, mister."

"What is this?" I cried for the hundredth time that night. I watched as the sun vanished again behind clouds of smoke. Was this really the new normal of the world?

We were back in the booth.

Our cups were refilled and she closed her eyes, her fingers drummed on the small giftwrapped box in front of her.

"It's for that girl again, isn't it? I've seen the way she's looked at you. It makes me smile." I sipped my coffee. "I bet you check your phone a dozen times to see if she's called."

She gazed into my eyes. "Why do you keep coming back to this place if you hate it so much?" she asked me.

"The coffee isn't strong, it just took too long to get here," I replied.

"It's for the beautiful cook with the snake tattoo across her chest."

"If you drink it with cream and sugar, it's not too bad,"

"It's the tattoo I like the best."

"How do you know she's got a tattoo there?"

She changed the subject.

It was getting convoluted. The narrative was breaking down. Soon, we would be jabbering nonsense for the sake of scaring off silence. She lifted her shirt and began to slip cutlery into her waistband. She winced as a steak knife cut her skin. "Pain is good for the soul," she said through closed teeth.

I stood and gathered my sheaves of paper. "It's time to go," I said, and walked for the door. I gave my head a shake and wondered what alarms and whistles and bells would go off on the other side. I seemed to smell the betrayal, the feeling of an old enemy returning to storm the gates. I would watch for a dying ember between lying lips.

It all shifted again. NO DRINKS BEYOND THIS POINT. The sign screamed at me from the wall of this new enclosure.

This fancy room was not for me. I prefer to find a quiet little shitter in the city for the winter, where I could do my lines and pass my time.

I stood and the floor rose up to meet my feet. The strange lights reflected from the pennies on the floor. They were thrown down yesterday. They're not worth anything anymore.

The little imperfections jump out at you first. The chips of paint, the cigarette burns on the chairs, the coats of arms above the doors. What you don't really have is really what you see.

I smiled. Would they miss that painting hanging on the wall? It wouldn't be too hard to steal it. I just love taking pictures.

But I don't want that picture. I want a black daisy, or a grey rose. I want to see a flower bleed.

It's a bit easier to focus now. The paranoia's dying down. I can enjoy the misconceptions better, now that I can hear the whispers.

A small sip of water would be excellent, and a glass of wine would be such bliss. It was something I thought I would never miss. Like an Irish bard, I began to sing at the stall wall.

"I've seen you falter and I've seen you break
I've seen you take chances you were
never meant to take
I cannot be certain
What exactly has made you hurt,
But give 'em hell
And time will tell."

We stepped through a window into the sunlight. She walked along the wall, pretty as lingerie on a mannequin devoid of sex. Snowflakes fell upon her, and she knew that the rain will rust her armour and the sun will pale her to the point of no return.

I could see that she was walking wounded into a crowd of the young and the stupid. Nothing was going to save her now, not even me.

I couldn't leave this space. I needed to stay right there and never move. The change would've been too drastic. My mind had lost its elasticity and couldn't stretch to fit in any new information.

I could see the spider on the ground. It had three dozen legs and fourteen heads and it was spinning its web toward me.

I started to dig a trench around me. I piled the dirt up to surround me. Here's hoping it couldn't cross the ditch, but it did. "Shit! Go away! Go away! Please make it go away!" I screamed. I smashed it with my fist. It was made of nothing, and that was exactly what I missed.

"We dug down deep that day, hoping for water," I giggled maniacally. "We only found oil." I rubbed the dirt onto my face, as they had trained me to do. "Most of the men wanted to hold onto it, screaming that we were now rich. 'We're in the desert', I said. 'If it makes you so rich, then drink it and see how wealthy you feel.'"

"Don't stop now," she said. "We're almost there. See that light in the forest? That is where we are heading."

One step after another. I had hair down to the shoulders. She spun it into curls.

"When that rifle crack echoes through quiet poplars, and you exhale that breath you've been holding, the steam from your exhalation mingles with the muzzle smoke in the frigid air above your head. It's only then that you feel the cold once again, as you head towards the kill."

"Walk away from it, Soldier Boy. Old soldiers die lonely, and young soldiers die quick. Write on paper, leave it in the trees," she said, soothingly. "Touch the branches and walk away."

I kissed her on the lips. "You have no idea how much you've influenced me, old heart," I said. "Hold the line together. Let's hold it as its burning."

The night she beat to death the dogwood tree was the same night we danced around the fire. We burned the books that held the numbers. Like children, we spun in circles. We sang old songs written by dirty hippies.

"Sky dancer in the morning light,
I've been waiting for you
We have a mutual friend in the rain
When can I see you again?"

What has brought us here, to the edge of reason, to the brink of blindness? This is your proof that there is no god, no pearly gates, and no chosen son. If there was, he would not let you have slipped away from me.

More dirty hippy songs.

"Sky dancer, afternoon delight

It breaks my heart to see you from so far away
I wanted to kiss and tell you
I want to touch and smell you
Tell me bedtime stories all along the way."

I watch my movies in black and white. I sometimes wish that I could do the same in real life. It would clear a lot of things up for me. You'll never know a TV screen that has gone to snow as the station went off the air. What a shame. It's one more loss to the world of White Noise. It's a sinking boat on a murky inland sea. Do you want to talk about it? Yeah, I didn't think so.

I rubbed my eyes until they stung. I was craving breakfast from a greasy trucker dive. The last time I tried to eat there, they told me they didn't serve my kind. When I asked for clarification, I was hit with a steel pipe from the gas jockeys.

I tried to write haiku once. I failed miserably in the attempt. Is this what I have been reduced to? It's far too late to sleep, but it's way too early to be awake. If I close my eyes for a moment, will she come back and whisper in my ear and tell me what I need?

I've never been in this room before, although I've lived here going on to 15 years. Wonders never cease to amaze me. All this smoke, all this brimstone, and it's mine? These newspaper clippings, they cover the walls like a bad rash.

Somewhere, out a window, in a bedroom, the sight unseen, I hear a bass line of a song I haven't heard since I was 14.

I start to hum the melody as I scratch my nails on the wall. I peel and scrape at the ancient news. It crumbles to the floor.

The dust and decay make me weep as it gets into my eyes. I miss my uniform sleeve. It was perfect for wiping away tears.

"Sir, are you okay?"

The waitress taps my shoulder. She has my bill in her hands. I look down at the table. My pages are torn and shredded. I look around. Nothing has changed. I scan the restaurant for the purple faux-fur coat. I see nothing.

"Sir?" she says again. The fear in her face drips down her nose and onto the tabletop.

I look her square in the eye. "The girl, where did she go?"

"What girl?" she asked. Her voice cracked.

I stare down at the booth. "The one who was sitting right there, where did she go?"

Her frightened and blank expression told me that I would never set foot in this place again. I pulled $20 from my wallet. "You creep the hell outta me, lady," I heard myself say, "far more than any ghosts. How many cigarettes do you need to smoke for your mouth to look like that?"

She moved to say something, but I stopped her. "Speak not, and forever hold your teeth." I picked up my coat and ran outside. I ran the few blocks to my squalid room. I scaled the stairs and locked the doors behind me as I went. Once I reached my room, I slammed my door and pressed my back to it. Silence.

By then, I was crawling around on my hands and knees, looking on the floor for any words I may have missed, searching for scraps of paper that my muse may have kissed. I noticed that my writing was messy, and my tired eyes began to fail.

"Damn me to hell," I cried out, "but only if they'll take me. I know that if I stay here, fate won't hesitate to rape me." This literary jerking off began to cramp my wrists. I didn't want to, but my restless mind insisted.

I saw it there; that key, that goddamn skeleton key. I was incredulous. How dare you mock me? Listen, I write for me, not for you. I write what I feel. Even this feels foreign to me. Since when do I answer to you?

I caught my breath and stuck my hands into my pockets. It was then I felt the cubes. Many of them. Lots of them. Enough to destroy minds until the end of the world. They were there, along with the skeleton key.

There was a knock at the door, just as the first dose of cubes was dissipating, and just as I remembered an old tattoo I once had on my leg. It's been gone a long time; the tattoo, not the leg.

I opened the door to the extent of the chain. She stood there; her fake blonde hair plastered to her head.

"It's cold. Let me in," she said, her voice gravelly.

I did as she asked.

She lit a smoke as she sat down on my couch. I stood with my back against the door. She had turned up at the door of the Temple, her hair was soaked with rain. They had offered her a towel, then closed the door again.

"So," I began, but she glared at me.

"I said I was cold, and you hoped I would freeze,' she said curtly. "You contract and expand like the light of a match. I sent you a message, and yet I knew you would not reply."

I held up the key. "This?" I asked.

She nodded and lit another smoke. "Pluck a rose and it stays pretty until the time death catches up with it." She stood and wrapped her arms around me.

I looked down the cleavage of sweet broken dreams, and I knew. It was time to leave this chamber. It was time to leave the den.

CHAPTER 2

What wise man brought this foolishness to our door? What humble sage said, "This is a good idea?" Is he the fool for saying it, or are we the fools for listening? Perhaps we should've paid closer attention. Perhaps we should have listened closer.

I put the book and pen down, stood and stretched. I glanced at the clock that hung on the far wall. Its hands showed that it was approaching midnight. I walked over to another stack of books. At the very top of the pile, I found the book I was looking for; well-read and dog-eared, like so many others scattered in heaps throughout the cavernous and dark warehouse. I tried to reach it with my hands, but the stack was taller than me, and the book was just out of reach. I looked around the shoreline of the island of light I stood in, and, just outside the circle, I saw the handle of a push broom.

I picked up the broom, and with the softest of sighs, I swung the bristled head of the broom like an axe towards the stack of books.

It connected with a dull thud, and once again, books rained down, pages falling out of the spines and fluttering like leaves. Some books skittered across the concrete floor; those that bore the hit flew farther across the room.

Inertia kept the top books from flying away. They dropped onto the pile with a thud. I dropped the broom and bent over to pick up the book that I had reached for.

It was old, and the leather cover had developed such a curvature that it almost looked as if the book had been soaked in water. Perhaps it had, I didn't know. I walked over to my chair and sat down again. I opened the cover and read a few of the lines.

"Words of old are wasted on the new..."

I tore the page out and crumpled it up, throwing it into the darkness.

"Words cannot die, words are always there..."

I tore this page out as well.

"My words are forever..."

I tore this page out, too.

"My words are holy..."

I disgustedly lobbed the book in the direction of the delivery doors. I heard the metallic bang and the echoing rattle as the book hit the doors. The sound carried throughout the room.

I scratched my chin. Not much longer, I thought. I stood and stepped over books and papers, careful not to step on anything and slip. I walked to where the light glinted off the handle of a hand-jack.

I pumped the handle down three or four times, the weight on the other end of little concern. I took hold of the handle and began to pull it towards the easy chair. As it moved into the light, I smiled.

The smooth mahogany finish of the casket was immaculate, without a blemish or so much as a fingerprint to mar its lustre.

The chrome handles shined in the 60-watt glow of the swag lamp. I knew that the interior was lined with the finest silk and velvet. Such care and craftsmanship went into building this fine container, and its sole purpose was to be filled with a decaying corpse and to be buried six feet underground forever. It was a waste.

I released the handle of the hand-jack. The forks sank to the ground with a hydraulic hiss. I walked over to the front of the coffin and opened the lid. I looked at the contents and smiled.

I turned from the casket and walked to a bookcase. Normally, this bookcase would stand flat against a wall, but this bookcase stood out in the middle of the floor.

I picked up a flashlight that sat on one of the shelves and turned it on. I trained its beam to the chaos and disorder of the papers on the shelves. I rifled through until I found the items that I was looking for.

I took a well-worn leather book from the shelf, as well as several other papers and notes. Turning the flashlight off, I turned back towards the chair. I sat down with my papers and sighed.

On the small table beside my chair was a simple white china tea service. I gazed upon the service for a moment, then, with a sweep of my hand, I swept the service onto the floor. The china shattered on the concrete, bits skittering into the darkness.

I moved the table to just in front of the chair. I transferred the paperwork from my lap to the table top, and, picking up the pen and ink, I began to write once again.

'The Twelve Steps of Stupidity.
Difference to ignorance
Ignorance to fear
Fear to ego
Ego to thought
Thought to like-minded individuals
Like-minded individuals to hate
Hate to retribution
Retribution to counteraction

Counteraction to war
War to death
Death to burial customs
Burial customs to difference'

It sounded like madman's folly. This notion of "I am the fight", with its aura of Guerrilla tactics falling before my teary eyes.

The idea being that the only great ones are the dead ones. Why does greatness come at the price of my life? If to be immortalized means that I must die, so why don't I? Is it philosophy as simple as "to thine own self be true" all that kept me alive thus far?

How many times did I stand there and watch as younger eyes than mine stared up at me for the answer on how to make it out alive? "I am not a holy man," I would scream. "Don't you dare make a god out of me!"

I made the most out of it all and, when the wheel turns, here's hoping I'll have my lessons down, because, if reincarnation is real, the penance will be a real bitch.

When it all went up in flames that day, I stood and watched it burn. I could care less…or could I?

Those of us on the outside are waiting. We stood and waited. I tried to stand in the crowd and watch. I stayed left of centre and the human tides swirled around me. They swerved to avoid, their eyes never met mine, save for the young ones, they will always stare, because they see in us what they want to be. Our reality is their desire. They pretend to be us on playgrounds and in toy rooms. We could be gods among mortal men, but we should not impose. It wouldn't be...right.

You must make your fellow man uncomfortable at least once a day. Patience is a virtue that is a cruel mistress. She is a mental cock-tease that drives you mad. It leaves you second guessing and impulse shopping while you are alone with your thoughts. You change and you curse and you invocate, only to realize that there is a fine line between poetry and bitching.

Once upon a time, I had carved into the frame above my door. CARPE MORTE. Seize the Dead. It seems to me that it had meant something at some point, or perhaps not. Perhaps it was a feeling that all was not well in the universe at that particular moment. I was, and still am, afflicted with a kinetic convex that forces me to assume the emotions of others and wear them upon my sleeve. I had become a cosmic dumping ground for discarded emotions, like a food bank collection bin where some asshole has left dented cans of dog food and called it charity.

Those days were gone, and now my own expanses were my bread and butter. Now I am left with a pile of papers.

♦ ♦ ♦

I stopped and stared down at my lap. I saw that I had come to the last page in the ledger.

I stood and looked around the warehouse, knowing full well that there was a similar book somewhere amongst the chaos.

I found it tucked under my chair. A smile came to my face, but it quickly dissipated when I opened the front cover. While I could have dealt with the musty smell, the fuzzy patches of black and blue and green and grey that engulfed the majority of the pages had rendered it useless.

"Shit," I said, and, like a discus, I hurled the mouldy ledger off towards some dark corner of the warehouse. I could hear it slap against the floor.

A flash of insight came. I stepped over the scattered piles of books and approached a narrow set of cement stairs that ascended towards the offices of the warehouse.

The heels of my shoes scraped slightly on the rough cement steps. At the top, a heavy steel fire door stood to my right. I opened it and stepped inside.

The red fire exit sign bathed the corridor in crimson light. Doors to the left and to the right of me opened to small offices. I breezed past the first two sets of doors and stopped at the third door on the right-hand side. A small sign said "Accounting." I opened the door.

The room was dry and stale. A metal office desk squatted on the floor, next to the remains of a rodent-eaten upholstered office chair. Piles of shredded paper were scattered through the room, and stacks of file folders stood sentinel in the corners.

I walked over towards where a large sheet metal cabinet stood, its doors closed. I stepped towards the cabinet, and from under my foot came the distinct sound of crushing ceramic. In the pale emergency lights, I could make out the remains of a broken white ceramic coffee mug that once bore the image of the cartoon character Ziggy.

I opened the cabinet doors and my smile returned. Protected from the mice and from the mould stood a stack of long ledger books. I counted seven of them in total. I lifted them out of the cabinet and returned to my chair.

I opened the ledger on the top of the pile. The first three pages were filled with figures. I tore these pages from the ledger and threw them on the floor, leaving fresh pages.

The bookcase beckoned me once again. A wooden box that once held a set of silver cutlery sat upon one of the shelves. Inside were dozens of military medals, from different nations and different conflicts. The light gleaned upon them as if they were gold coins in a pirate's hoard. I ran my hands lovingly across the medals. I began to pick medals from the box, and pin them to my shirt. British service medals clinked against Iron Crosses and American medals of honour. I was festooned with decorations from combative states spanning most of the 20th century.

A shuffling from the darkness caught my attention. I looked up. The flutter of a pigeon up in the rafters. The bird, with the oil slick neck markings hardly visible from the pool of light, was flying vainly above, desperately searching for a means of exiting the darkened warehouse.

It landed on a steel girder, flew away again, circled around in the air momentarily, and then landed once again on the girder. The pigeon sidestepped to its right four or five times before it began to defecate.

The white globular masses of shit fell onto the polished lid of the coffin, the dull thump thump thump barely audible.

I looked forlornly at the once pristine lid of the coffin that was now marred. I sighed and stared at the mess for a few minutes. It began to run like candle-wax down either side of the rounded top, stopping after a few inches as it congealed.

I stared at the shit as it rolled down the sides of the coffin lid. I was lost in the middle of a daydream, my mind far away from the little bird and the mess that it had made. My mind was miles from the warehouse and the chair and the ledgers and the mountains of books. My mind was lost in the fog of time.

I remembered when I first heard the voice of the Muse inside my head. In my mind's eye, we sat at a poker table. She was dressed as an Old West whore.

"My silence shocked you," she said. "I'm in here waiting. I'll come and see you when you are weakened."

She found me sitting alone in the dark surrounded by ten thousand ghosts. "This cannot be the best you hoped for," she teased. "But it's what you got. Knowing I'm there and I'm gnawing away at your soul. Well, what do you do about it?" She pulled out a deck of cards. "I'll give you a choice boy," she said. "Dry tears don't take you very far. Prayers to an empty room are pointless. I can make it all go away, just come out and play."

"I've beaten you once," I said, thinking back to the days before I ran.

"But I'm still around," she said.

"I have all my friends," I said.

"They have their own crutches," she replied.

"I still have my mind," I said.

"But your heart, I have weakened," she said. She began to stack poker chips. "Tell you what," she said. "I see your 17 years and I'll raise you 10 and 1 more for good measure." She threw the chips into the middle of the table. "It's my pot to break," she said. "Your body is broken and your friends are all dead. What more do you have?"

I folded before a card was played.

I was proud. It had been good work, and this act of writing it all down each time the deed was done gave the whole thing a sense of completion, as if it wasn't really over and completed until I had written it down. And as the final words were scratched on the paper, I smiled at sat back.

A ticking sound caught my attention. I looked skyward to the pipes and wiring that snaked and crisscrossed the ceiling and the steel beams above. The ticking came from the pipes, expanding as hot water passed through them.

It reminded me of the sound of water dripping in a cave. Thirst inducing audio.

I walked over to a tall chest of drawers, upon which stood a wine glass of generous depth and a large bottle of whiskey. Unscrewing the cap, I poured the liquor into the wine glass, filling it almost to the top. I took four small sips of the whiskey, and, after studying the wine glass for a moment, quaffed the entire goblet of whiskey in one shot.

I picked up the ledgers and carried them over to the big steel loading bay door that faced the outside. I placed them on the floor in front of the door, one beside the other. I carried the chair over to the loading bay door, and set it down facing the door. I situated the chair until it faced due east, directly in the middle of the loading bay door.

My hand reached into my pocket. There were still several cubes. I took one from my pocket, and held it up to the light, like a jeweller inspecting a gem.

They weren't much to look at, not much bigger than a sugar cube, but then, that is the design upon which they were based. They were meant to look like sugar cubes, those mind-expanding sugar cubes the longhairs gobbled all those years ago. Christ, if those dirty hippies even knew what was coming.

I still am not quite sure how she got a hold of these things, but then, it was probably for the best that I didn't know. I closed my eyes and slipped one onto my tongue.

It was nearly dawn when the door to the outside opened with a creak.

She stood erect, her eyes darting left and right, scanning the recesses of the warehouse. She walked towards the island of light, stepping lightly over the shattered glass and scattered books, her hands jammed into her purple fur coat.

The figure moved with great poise, far more than she had ever shown before. She was regal, her face stoic.

Her lips parted softly as she spoke. "At last, I have found you." She turned and scanned the darkness. "I found your message, written on the wall in that alley."

My voice boomed out from the darkness. "Weeks."

She turned to face the voice. "Has it been that long?" she asked.

"Yes, it has."

She smiled a sad smile. "It doesn't seem that long, does it?"

"It has to me."

"I guess my gauge of time is off."

I stepped out of the darkness. I stood with my hands behind my back. "Do you know why I've brought you here?" I asked.

She looked at me, her mind somewhere else. "I have a pretty good idea"

I stepped towards her until we were mere inches apart.

She looked up into my face. Her eyes met mine. We stared for several heavy moments, searching each other's eyes for the answers we both sought.

It was she who broke the spell. "You've changed. Your eyes, they are so hard, so…"

"…broken?" I offered, finishing her sentence.

She smiled. "I wouldn't say that." She took hold of my shoulders. Pulling me in, she kissed me deeply, our tongues dancing within each other's mouths.

I pulled away and smiled.

"Did you miss me?" She asked. Her voice was sultry and inviting.

I closed my eyes and stepped back. "I did, several times, in fact."

I lifted her chin. Looking down at her, I smirked. "Look at you. You're helpless, maimed, and begging. Shall I put you out of your misery, right here and now?" I swung towards her face. The book I held in my hands stopped mere inches from her forehead. She winced, then blinked. I dropped the book and kicked it away. "No, you have toyed with me for far too long, and now, it is my turn."

I walked over to the casket, throwing open the lid.

"That cannot harm me," she laughed out. "You know that! None of this can harm me."

I spoke. "Mine is not to harm. I have set my trap, and you have taken the bait. My mission is nearly complete." I led her to the casket. "Get in, quickly," I told her.

She hesitated, but then stepped into the silk lined box. Inside were dozens of skeleton keys, of different shapes and sizes. She lay down upon them.

I reached into my hip pocket and withdrew a gold pocket watch. I opened it and smiled. "It is nearly time," I said to her.

"Nearly time for what?" she whispered at me. "What are you doing?"

I walked over to the side of the loading bay door, where the controls for the automatic door opener hung. The controls had enough slack cable to reach from the wall to the casket. The control box was steel, with two buttons coloured red and green.

I looked at the pocket watch again. It said 6:59 AM.

"It's time," I whispered into her ear. I opened her mouth and slid all of the small cubes inside. I closed the lid of the casket.

When the time turned to seven AM., I took a deep breath and pressed the green button on the control box.

The overhead door mechanism, long disused, screeched and groaned in protest as its chains and gears turned hard, pulling the heavy door skyward. The rubber gasket at the bottom of the bay door had adhered itself to the concrete floor, and for the briefest of moments, it held firm, until the force of the door pulling broke it free with a rubbery schlock.

The door opened a few inches, and the first rays of the morning sun spilled into the warehouse in a semicircle of light. As the door opened wider, the semicircle of light grew larger, inch by inch.

The sunlight soon crept up across the ledgers as they lay on the floor. The light crept in farther and farther, until it soon reached the legs of the chair. It was going to be a beautiful day.

CHAPTER 3

In the tomb she stumbled, tripping over ancestors long dead and forgotten. Her only illumination the cigarette lighter held in front of her.

The lock had given easy. Old metal breaks under new crowbar.

Moving through the dust and the mould in the clammy air of the marble hole, she searched for the letter that she had written so long ago. It was written on good paper and rolled up with black ribbon. "Dear granny," scrawled in a child's hand, "they say you are dead. What does that means? They won't tell me. Why won't you wake up and play with me?"

She falls and slams her knees into the corner of a heavy wooden box. Stilettos were never made for walking on the mouldy marble floor of a crypt. The pain is glorious, seemingly lighting the tomb. She curses and swears, but then looks around to see if the dead have been offended.

She finally reaches the box that she's after.

It's still there, on top of Granny.

A smile and a tear come to her overdone face. Her fingers tremble as they reach for it. Closer, closer…

The gentle touch has been too much, and the paper crumbles. The dead have been disturbed for nothing.

She begins to curse herself in the guise of the crumbled paper. "Naïve little stupid bitch," she hisses. "You wouldn't know what to do with me if you tried. I would be turned over in your hand several times, a cursory glance around to see who was watching, and then, unceremoniously dumped to the ground again."

The sound of the night watchman approaching with his baying hound sent her back to Grandmother's side.

"Many try, and many do fail. Those who are too afraid sit and watch; wondering waiting, hoping."

The hound bayed once more. "The wild dogs howl around me," she whispered to her grandmother, "like some demented choir in a cathedral long abandoned by the parishioners."

She huddled deeper in the shadow. "They come in closer, granny. They can smell the fear in you, and the blood in me. I'll bet that they will attack you first. The fearful are much more fun than I. I am merely bleeding."

She pressed her lips close to the sealed edge of the coffin. "You will run, and you will hide. They will follow you. It is hide and seek for the ages. I will close my eyes here, and rest for a while under the tall wet grass and dripping leaves."

She could now hear the footsteps outside the vault. The sniffing of the dog grew louder.

She whispered still to the coffin. "You once asked how I knew of such things. The answer I gave was not to your liking. You said I was too young to speak the way I do. You said that you played for the love of the game. If that was the case, then why keep score?"

The beam of a flashlight slammed into her face. She stumbled backwards onto her purple coat. She held her hand up to push the light away. With a wavering voice, she began to sing:

"The fire is cold
And the embers stopped glowing
And yet we stare into the grey and white ash
Still drawing heat from so little
There is no more dry wood to burn
It is all green
And not ready for the fire."

The room was lit like the aisle floor of a midnight airplane. A softly lit path between the darkness. I began to follow the path into the darkness, my steps still not making a sound. I had gone about 12 feet when the lights came on above me. I was in a room filled from floor to ceiling with shelving, the sturdy metal shelving of a storage facility. The shelves were absolutely packed with objects that seemed like every audio-visual club from every elementary school in the province had been robbed and raided of everything they had ever owned for over fifty years. There were overhead projectors, slide projectors and reel-to-reel decks, film projectors and public-address speakers and microphone stands. Typewriters and monochrome computers, fax machines, teletype machines, and on and on. The shelves filled nearly every inch of the space.

Beyond it all, a door, and a stage.

I reached for the door handle, expecting the warmth I had felt the night before. Instead, the handle was cold, frigid, like grabbing a flagpole in winter with a bare hand. I pressed down on the thumb latch and pulled. The door didn't move. I tried again. Still nothing. The door was now locked. I pounded on the door. After a few moments, I pounded again.

It was then that I noticed a small metal box with a hinged cover attached to the wall, just beside the door around five feet up. I was almost certain that it was not there the night before. I lifted the cover. Inside was an intercom and a small surveillance camera. I pressed the button. "Hello?" I called into the intercom.

"State your business," said a voice.

I took a stab at it. What the hell, I thought. The bastards would never know about it, so why worry? It wasn't going to cost me anything, and besides, I had very little to lose at that moment. It's silly to think about it now, how goddamn terrified I had been about the whole thing. This kind of opportunity didn't present itself as often as I would've liked, but still, I was a little bit scared by it all.

"I want out of here," I replied. "Don't you know who I am?"

No reply.

I heard a voice in the darkness, though. A flame flickered.

He offered me a cigarette. I hadn't had one in a long time. I took it in my hand, and lit it. I twirled my hair nervously.

"You're fidgeting badly," he said to me in his thick Cockney accent. "Does it make your skin crawl? Do you turn away? Does it bother you that much?"

If the man had kept his teeth clean, or any part of himself clean, really. It would not have bothered me.

He took another drag. "I can see it," he said. "The sound of my voice makes you uncomfortable. You're terrified of me. Your stomach says run but your legs won't move, will they?" He exhaled a cloud of smoke. "Well, darling, if it gets any worse, you'll start to cry. Your lips will tremble and quiver. Your comfort zone will be breached, and I will inch forward towards you, my breath warm against you."

I looked around and could imagine the dead eyes staring back at me. The hum of the machinery somewhere deep inside the bowels of the building made the floor vibrate. The cube was wearing off by now. "Doesn't it bother you being here?" I asked.

He laughed. "What, in here?" he shook his head. "The setup is familiar, and the changes are slight. It makes one more careful, that's all. It makes you concentrate a little harder. It makes you step every step very carefully. I close my eyes against the night. I try to sleep, I try to rest, but the dead won't let me be." He pointed out towards the old machines. "They scream like playing children. Their dead eyes stare at me. They want and ask too much of me." He shook his head. "It used to be different. I used to say, 'Please go away, please leave me be. For the love of whatever god you pray to, find someone else, at least for one night,' but no, not this lot."

He walked over to the edge of the stage. He went to step down, but he missed the first step and fell the rest of the way.

I could hear his gasping breath, heard forever here now. I crawled on my hands and knees over to the edge.

Our glances met, and I froze.

He coughed and sputtered. "Bloody hell," he said, as he stared at his body as it vanished bit by bit. "There's nothing there, mate. There is no escape. The ghosts are here. This is their room; this is their space. Can you feel them staring?" He smiled as he vanished. "You will now, unless you got a key for that door."

I stood and stared at the darkness behind me. I ran into the black, my hands outstretched, unsure of what they would find in the darkness. They met brick; a good sign. Brick was good. Brick was real. It was tangible.

I felt the wall and soon found what felt like a light switch. I flipped it on.

A small red bulb illuminated an old wooden door. I reached for the handle and tried to pry the door open. It would not open. I began to pound upon the door, beating upon it with the heels of my hands.

I looked skyward and saw the letters scratched into the brickwork. How I smiled when I saw those words.

I reached into my pocket and pulled out that old skeleton key. "Hullo, Voodoo Queen!" I called out. "Big Mama," I said, "I got something here that you've been needing."

The key went in, and it turned like a charm. The door swung open, and I stepped inside.

Inside, however, was Outside, and it was Outside where I found her.

She wiped her eyes when she saw me. "Jesus Christ…"

I smiled. "No, I am not."

She tried to laugh, but she only cried some more. "I've been having bad dreams," she started to say, but she took to gasping hard and heavy. "At least I hope that they are bad dreams. God forgive me if this all turns out to be real."

I took her hand. "Tell me about them," I asked. I offered her one of the cigarettes I had left from the Man on the Stage.

She lit it. "I met the evil inside the common man," she began. "I shook his hand, and he made me sit down. He offered me food and wine. He gave me free choice of the women he had gathered there." Another drag on the smoke. "I shook my head to his offers. 'I am very particular with whom I break bread', said I, and had no desire to be taken into his confidence."

"Go on," I said.

She did. "He laughed at this, and called me a fool. 'Hundreds of others would sell me their souls to have the offer that I've made to you,' he said. I did not care, I said, and I stood to leave. Only then did I know that my eyes were still closed from when I went to sleep, and I couldn't wake up. I just couldn't wake up…"

The tears came again. Her purple fur coat was stained with mud.

I should have held her, soothed her, but I didn't. I stuck my hands in my pocket. "Do you wish we were still back at the coffee shop?" I asked her.

She looked up at me with her mascara streaked eyes. "Can we just go back to the beginning? Simply rewind the spool and start again? Will the gears catch, and will the great lumbering Machine return to the way it worked when it was new? Will the conglomerate of parts perform the tasks for which it was designed so very long ago? Will the answer be clear to me, now? What meant so much then and so little now. So simple, so plain. How foolish of me. Rest, sweet rest. Please bring me sweet rest."

I finally sat down in the muck beside her. "A sticky cog in the wheel of the Great Machine, running down the innocent and using their electrical life-force to power the engine. Sleep is meaningless," I said. "The nights spent dreaming; sleep does not mean rest. Not when you dream like I dream."

She looked at me. "How do you dream?" she asked.

I sighed. "I am a payphone on a busy corner, the receiver never hung up. I'm a nocturnal dispatch system. Basic motor skills function, you know. The odd intelligent word spills forth.

Once in a while, the muse steps out and kicks the tires. No slumber."

"Sweet slumber, but for a while," she murmured. "Let the ghosts find another channel tonight. Let me rest." She burrowed her head into chest and closed her eyes.

Have you ever watched someone as they slept? Peaceful, isn't it? Stare at their closed eyes. Wait for them to open and stare back at you. I watched her as she slept.

Had I loved her, I would've kissed each eyelid softly, gently, so as not to wake her. It seems like a romantic thing to do. I'd write poetry on her bare skin with my bare finger a mere breath from her skin, tracing the outline of handwritten words. Finally, I'd touch her. Perhaps she'd sigh, then roll over.

But I had been there before. Touched her face in the night, ran my fingers through her hair and told her that all will be well.

I almost listened to that little voice that said that she'd follow you to the ends of the earth, and she'd share the wine and break the bread, and she will love you.

That little voice never told me honest, though. It never said, "Walk slowly through it, do not rush. Enjoy this moment. It will never be this way again, and if you miss any moment of it. You can't turn right around and return to the beginning."

I knew that it will not work, at least if you are like me. I'd made that journey. My eyes are wide open now. I could not love her more, with senses on fire. It would be touch, taste, feel, and the words on the page would simply read, "She comes, she goes, she's gone."

She had given me an empty book. The pages were blank, fresh, clean, and pure. Virgin lines unspoiled by ink or stain.

"Are you sure about this?" I asked.

She smiled. "Yes, go on." She said.

"Where did you get this?" I asked.

No answer came from her. She stood and threw more wood on the fire.

I picked up the pen, opened the cover, and stopped.

"What is it?" she asked.

"There it is again," I said. "The hesitation to touch it. Like your very first time."

She looked at me with dull eyes.

"I'm unsure what to do with it," I said. "I'm afraid."

"Afraid of what?" she asked. "Are you afraid you might do something wrong? Afraid to mar the surface? To scratch pen upon it?" She cackled. "You're a chicken-shit. An unnatural fear. Relax, It's only paper."

I held it in my hands. "This trepidation, is it normal? Is it sane?"

She was getting angry with me now. "Are you afraid that you will waste it? It's meant to be drawn upon. What's the fear? It is merely an empty book."

"That is what logic would say," I said, "but if I listened to logic, I wouldn't have a library of virgin books in a box."

She ripped it from my hand and threw it in the fire. "And you spent all that time writing in those slimy ledgers." She said.

I watched as it burned.

"I write for me, not for you,' I hissed at her. "I write what I feel. If you like it, fine. If not, too bad."

She stepped towards me. "Do all words need reason? What about Ginsburg and the Old school? Even this feels foreign to me. Since when do I answer to you? Why do I defend myself? Have you attacked me? Are you my enemy?"

I laughed and pulled a cube out of my pocket. "What can be said and what can be had," I replied. I held it up. "What will you do with it? What will you do for it?"

She stopped short. She drove her hands deep into the pockets of her purple fur coat. "Turn lead into gold, I guess? A dream? Get rich quick the hard way. Rumpelstiltskin in the flesh." She crouched down by the fire, trying to get warm. "If you can impress me and succeed, then, by all means, glean the fillings from my teeth and take the strings from my guitar. Pull the bullets from my gun. Use all the metal that you can find." She poked the embers with a stick. "But fail, and you shall lose the faith," she said. "The fire will melt all that enters. Make what you will. Beat it with hammers and with stones but do not wait for abundance out of emptiness. Remember, what will come to pass will pass, or so the fates say. Cash your chips and walk."

I did not expect those words to come from her. She never struck me as the type. "I see within you a voice of reason," I said. "But you choose to ignore it constantly."

She held up a finger accusingly. "Mind my words and I will curse you," she replied. "I'm not here to teach. Merely to watch."

I felt that now was the time to ask her what I'd always wanted to ask, but never had the right moment. "Tell me about her," I asked.

She was silent for a long time before she spoke. She lit a cigarette. "We were drunk the last time I saw her," She said. "Our lips met in an awkward embrace under a streetlight. It was the moment that I had desired since the moment we first met."

"Then what happened?" I asked.

"My lost little bird slipped out of my grasp," she said softly. "I was not meant to hold her. We were glimmers of light in the darkness, flashing like sparks from funeral fires." She blew a plume of smoke. "The years passed, and I wondered where and what and when. My lost little bird… Around the world and back again. She never left my mind; always there, always wondering…She once was lost," she clutched the leather pouch at her neck. "But now she's found, my lost little bird of the shadows."

She was crying, but she hid it terribly. She wiped the tears from her eyes with the palms of her hands like a child. She stood up. "It's time," she said. "Put aside your innocent guise. Gather up these square little friends of ours. Go to where we can light the fire again. Tonight, we rise."

We took a wander through the graveyard at dawn. We could see the ravens perched upon the stones of those embalmed departed.

I tugged on her sleeve. "Do you think your Aunt would rest in peace if she knew a big black bird shit upon the granite slab she paid for?" I said.

She did not answer.

We walked to where water was being drawn from the earth. She stopped. "Walk to the well and peer down," she commanded.

I did, and saw my rounded reflection in the blackness.

"Does the earth shake just a little, as if she's trying to throw you in?"

I hadn't noticed until she told me, but it did.

"Vertigo," she called out. "Hang on to the stone lip. Close your eyes. Hold on. Let the world stop spinning. Feel the growing sense inside that there is very little to take away, like a forest falling under the blade of a madman's saw."

I continued to stare into the abyss.

"Don't let go," she called. "Let the pebbles under your feet fall for you. Sacrifice the little stones. Splash, splash, splash."

I reached down and did as she said. My reflection danced and bobbed with each stone.

I didn't know she'd hit me until she did.

A splash of cold water brought me around to my senses. I blinked as bright light and cold water filled my eyes.

I was lying flat on my back, on a very hard, very cold surface. The blinding light was directly above me, and, I could not see anything, but white light.

The echoing clicks of high heels on stone floor grew closer. I did not turn my head to see. I laid still, staring skyward.

"Is he awake enough?" a voice asked. It echoed and reverberated.

"I think so," answered another to the opposite side of me.

Curled up atop a marble tomb, sleeping with the eternally rested, sunlight streamed through the wrought iron gate. It caught me in the eye and woke me.

I shook the drunken glaze from my eyes. "The hair of the dog makes poor wool," I called out. "What's on tap at the top of the pile?"

My voice did not echo, but merely died upon the stone. "Ashes may come and dust may depart," I tried again, "but the chill remains in the vaulted arms of the mighty ones who stand watch over the dead."

The gate remained locked.

"Life amid the stones," I said as I sat down on the cold floor of the tomb. "Death around the bend."

She scribbled the words onto the paper, rapidly, like a maniacal scribe at the foot of a Mad King.

When she finished, she mumbled the words to herself out loud, to see how they sounded.

"Lover,
I've written hundreds of songs for you on a guitar I just realized has been slightly out of tune. I remember the way you taste, but don't hate me if your face escapes me. Songbirds sing, stealing tunes from other birds, or so it seems, and when the fancy takes me, I will let creativity run away.
If you love it, do it right and run away. Please don't hang your hopes upon a note or two, because music only makes sweet love when the singer gets paid.
Show me that this day is dragging, and I'll show you my road-weary smile. I anticipate the cold prairie night. By three AM, I will be gone. Everyone will be dead to the world and the world shall be mine."

She trembled as she read it. The paper rattled like the snake that it was.

The window slid up silently. Blessed are they who fear not the burglars.

Her green dress hung upon the wall. She slid beside her Lost Little Bird into bed and felt the warm spot where she had lain.

The Lost Little Bird rolled over and sighed before she hit her in the mouth, unknowing in her slumber.

Her lip bled onto the purple fur. "Serves me right for stealing her warmth," she whispered. "She's mean when she sleeps and I love it."

She cried for her; for others had and others would and some would try to take her away.

"Play with the words," she whispered into her ear. "They are to be enjoyed. Have your fun and let loose your mind. Your spirit will follow."

She was bitten and had bled, copper tasting, all but for a fleeting moment.

I tapped on the glass. She turned and scowled at me.

"What are you doing here?" She hissed.

"Why are YOU here?" I hissed back.

"So that my eyes can see and my mind can know," she whispered.

"Forget the time," I whispered. "Love her for now. The time will be short with her, a missed opportunity forever gone, and you shall weep inside for it. Let's flee."

She wept now. "This is the sign of love? Ecstatic bliss in the midst of sorrow? It'll break her soul in two tomorrow."

I reached my hand into the window. "Listen to the voice of reason," I pleaded. "The journey leaves much to be desired. Come with me. Let's ride this wind into tomorrow."

She looked at me. "Why should I?" she asked.

"I've gotten you this high," I replied. "I won't let you fall."

She laid the note upon the pillow before she slid out of the room.

CHAPTER 4

The Scene: a city bus.

"How did you escape the crypt?" She asked.

Gently I rubbed the bump on my head. "Only fitting," I smirked. "I locked you in a coffin full of keys, and you locked me in a crypt full of locks."

The bus hit a pothole and jolted us. I continued. "I could begin to see myself there, hiding away until the day is done, waiting for darkness to fill my need."

She snorted. "Abstract words for abstract minds: caress, digress and digest the rest, but please, carry on."

I did. "I faked rest with half closed eyes, pretending to dream of rituals of old. Those long drawn out affairs beneath the boughs of the gifting tree where even the mosquitoes are sacred." I yawned towards the window. "That's when I saw them."

She turned her head and blinked.

"The elemental ones, the pagans in the moonlight," I answered her unspoken question. "Their broadsword glinting in the candlelight, their incense hanging in the sacred circle with their nymphs darting into the night." I stretched in my seat. "They came to commune with the great night winds and to dance among the black trees and headstones. I watched them sway in the wind like madmen."

"So how did you escape?" she pressed.

I reached into my pocket and showed her my hand. "I bribed them with sugar cubes. They thought they held magic." I smiled. "You can always count on witches having a ritual in a graveyard to take candy from strangers."

We sat in silence for the next few miles. My mind however, was a dervish. I have seen the magic of a little black book. I have seen the medicine in empty lines and bare pages. The book has the power to make young girls smile and the paper makes them live. The paper gives birth to the poets within. They make themselves well. Their words heal and their words scream.

The book makes a grown man feel; where emotions stifled years before cry to be heard. Grown men cry and light up like an epiphany, and the book becomes gold. The book is their soul. I have seen the power of a little black book.

Inspiration took me now as it did back then. Borrowed muses and opportunity fleeting.
I coveted the Canadian mystics. I wanted to be Neil Young. I wanted to be Joni Mitchell and Leonard Cohen. I wanted my words to mean something.

"I wrote for the ghosts once," I mumbled. "They gave me stanzas to share. 'Too esoteric', it was said."

She was asleep beside me.

"I shall not seek you in Judea, but in the land of Shiva, where the tea flows darker than at home." The Hippie screamed out at the crowd in the firelight. "No gods will save me, no dead men nailed to trees. I do not seek it; I have no blind faith, nor do I respect based solely on age or foolish holiness!"

He jumped onto the roof of the car and held up his hands. "Honour and respect are earned through actions and deeds and character!" The Hippie shouted. "I will not bow in reverence because others tell me to!" He began to jump up and down upon the roof of the car. "My destiny is my own! My salvation my own concern! And when tomorrow turns into today I master my own fate!"

It was at this point, he was dragged away and beaten to death with hardcover copies of Sunday School Stories and rolled up newsletters.

I turned away from the window where I had been watching, as the bus passed by the scene.

An old woman sat and stared out the window a minute longer than I did. "Do you want to know the future?" She asked me.

She gently read my tarot. She said she knew my future, but I didn't believe her, but I listened very closely, so that I didn't offend her.

I give her silver trinkets and I thanked her for her reading. That's when I saw the soldier that was tattooed on her ankle.

I asked her why she had it, and she said that it's her father who was fighting in Korea when she was just a baby.

I can tell he didn't make it as she took her linen hemline and she covered up the drawing.

I said that I was sorry, and she said that I was forgiven, but I could feel my body swelling. I knew my throat was closing and I hoped that she will help me, but I knew that I'd be gone soon.

Suddenly, I was craving. I hadn't in a long time. That's when I knew it was all was an illusion. There was no old woman with a tattoo on her ankle.

By then the craving vanished, but I knew it would be back, so I closed my eyes, and I watched as the morning light lifted as I walked into the parlour. The tattoo guns were buzzing and recipients were screaming.

I told the pretty lady that I want to get a Romani woman.

She asked me, "Where do you want it?"

I told her, "on my ankle."

She smiled.

I was smiling as the bus slammed to a halt, and I was thrown to the floor.

CHAPTER 5

The Scene: another room.

I had caught a glimpse of where I was from under my blindfold.

The building was made of stone- field stones, set in mortar and cement. It was a square, squat little box, with not a window nor a decorative touch added to it. The door to the structure was exactly like the fire doors that I had in my high school. They were solid steel, their brown paint chipped and peeling, revealing the blue-grey metal beneath. A single orange exterior light buzzed over the door frame.

"Damn, boy! You wore the smile of a liar in the midst of a scam, and I knew damn well the game you were playing. But guess what, Junior, you're far from the first one to try and pull the wool over my eyes." The Sergeant chuckled. "I have forgotten more tricks and slight-of-hand than you will ever learn. Save your hustles for the tourists, buddy. Your bird don't fly here." He poked me with a finger. "Do you know what you are?"

"I know not what I am," I finally said.

The buzzing of the florescent lights was a torture of the Inquisition. The hard-wooden bench of the holding cell was no place to try and sleep, so the prisoners, all of us, sat upright. No one dared fall to the stone floor.

The crazy man beside me swayed. "My eyes keep me a simple history upon the back of a forgotten man," he said. "Lord Almighty, King Jesus, in Your name, I pray for my young son here." His calloused hand fell upon my shoulders, and his dead white eyes stared into the cosmos. "Get your feet wet, son, don't be afraid," he said, his hand on my shoulder. "The Lord won't hurt you. Memory can bullshit with the best of them. Run away from here. Dance, spin faster, faster, spin with the music, spin with the fire." He began to stomp his foot and clap his old hands together and mumble an old Southern Baptist hymn. "Spin with the turning of the Wheel, think of time and think of Jesus."

He stopped only when the rush had died. "You know," he whispered in my ear. "Hanged men would climax as the rope tightened. Can you imagine dying with cum in your shorts?" He then began to sing again in his Southern Baptist style.

It is March 20th, I think.

It's been a while since I've written anything. I've wanted to write, and I have so much to say about everything that has happened to me over the past few months, but hell, even getting paper and pens into here has been a struggle. Besides, I've struggled to know even where to begin. How does one begin a story like this? Who the hell in their right mind would even believe me? I mean, Jesus Christ, if you had gone through it, would you even want to try and remember it, let alone write it down?

The nights are calm here, at least. That's a good thing. The winds are cool, and they bring the smell of the salt air into the room. I wish I could leave, though. Jesus, do I wish I could leave, but it will be a long time before I can leave; if I'm ever allowed to leave here.

The room they keep me in is far from the cramped prison cell that I had when I first got here. The floors are always warm, and it is peaceful.

But I am getting ahead of myself. Out of context, you probably have no idea what I am talking about, right? I'll try my best to fill you in, but please, do not take what you are about to read as gospel. They messed with my memory so horribly in the beginning that even I doubt all of it happened as I think I remember.

That's the problem with this place. Time is messed up, and you have to really concentrate and focus on the order in which things actually happened, only to fail miserably.

The chair in the examination room was cold and unfriendly, just like the doctor before me.

"Tell me about the cubes," he said.

I sat in the chair, naked under the lights. "A man kills his brother and takes his wife. The son finds out, and acts fucking nuts. Everybody dies in the end." I said.

"I beg your pardon?" the doctor asked.

"Hamlet in a nutshell," I replied.

The doctor frowned as he scribbled. "Lieutenant," he said, "It's been nearly two years since your desertion. I want to know about those two years. For instance, when did you first find the cubes?"

I perched upon my chair. "Was it good for you?" I asked.

"What?" the doctor replied.

"Did you enjoy the play?"

"What play?" he asked.

"Where three million died for the King's suicide?" I said, making the sign of the cross. "Only then did they change the tune to the drums of war."

"I think we're done for the day..." the doctor began.

"I read the letter first before sending it back," I said. "'Dear mother, having a wonderful time. I shot a man in the head today. His clothes were different than mine. Have you taped my favourite shows while I have been away?'"

"That's quite enough," the doctor said.

"Where is the girl?" I asked.

He stopped. "The girl?" he said back to me. "The girl is of no concern to you. Now, if you wish to talk about your involvement..."

"My involvement?" I interjected. "You ask me to describe myself. What are you expecting, friend? Are you looking for the banners and stoic faces of long dead soldiers? Or do you seek in me the strength of will that pain breeds?" I stood naked before him. "Tell me, friend, what do you think of the Dead Man?"

He stood to leave but I barred his way. "Ask me of love, of life," I said. "Of what it is to see the world through eyes innocent and guilty. Let me show you my visions, not just my nightmares. Are you willing, friend?"

"That's enough, Lieutenant!" he shouted. "Guards!"

The door opened and I was thrown to the ground. Pinned down, I screamed at the top of my lungs, "I'm here to serve the King of Kings, but what of the Queen? Give me the Empire's rise! Give me Dominion Absolute! We'll save a fortune on election signs!" With that, I began to sing the Southern Baptist Hymn of the blind man. "Spin with the turning of the Wheel, think of time and think of Jesus."

The Scene: a different room.

The door opened, and the two nurses stepped into the room.

"How long has she been like this?" asked the nurse with only one eye.

"Since she arrived," replied the younger one. "They found her like this. She was hiding in the graveyard, beside the tomb of her grandmother."

She sat there in the middle of the floor, tearing to pieces the purple fur coat. She wore nothing but a hospital gown, her hair hung over her eyes. Her lips mumbled and her makeup smeared as she slowly began to turn feral. "Break, breaking, broken, broken, breaking, break, broken..." She pulled at the fur, tearing it from the sleeves as if plucking a chicken. Her voice softly began to become singsong as she pulled. "It broke, it broke. Breaking, broken. You broke it. You broke it." She soon began to scold herself. "Why did you break it? Breaking, broken." She began to sob. "She broke my heart. Break."

"Poor child," the one-eyed nurse said, and touched her lightly on the head. A flash of teeth, and the nurse retreated, her bitten hand cradled in the other.

The anger gone in a moment, she returned to pulling the fur from her coat and mumbling. "Broken glass, broken needle, broken record, break..."

The one-eyed nurse looked down at her hand. The skin wasn't broken, but the bruise would remain for a month. "Well," she said with Edwardian contempt. "Have the doctors seen her?"

The young nurse shook her head. "They are waiting for the effects to wear off," she replied. "She swallowed the rest of the cubes when the police apprehended her."

"Good Lord!" the one-eyed nurse exclaimed. "How many was there?"

Before the young nurse could answer, a shriek bellowed forth from the pile of fur. "Breaking the bank! Breaking her heart! Breaking her cherry! Break! Broken!"

The one-eyed nursed turned to the younger one. "I think it's time to bring in Mr. Price," she said.

"Mr. Price?" the younger nurse said in trepidation. "Are you sure?"

The one-eyed nurse nodded her head. "Now is the time," she replied, "when she is open to suggestion."

The younger nurse cleared her throat. "So, you do not wish to wait for the doctor?" She asked.

"No, I do not," replied the one-eyed nurse. She opened the door behind her. "Run along now," she commanded the younger nurse. "Leave us."

The younger nurse looked mournfully at the girl on the floor and shook her head. She did not say a word, but closed the door behind her.

"Breaking ground, Breaking wind," she bellowed from the pile of fur. "You broke it! It broke! It's broken! Break! Breaking! Broken!" She began to bawl.

The one-eyed nurse crouched down beside her. "Shhh," she said softly, "It's going to be okay."

The girl leaned her head onto the one-eyed woman's chest. She was like a child, her scrambled mind awash with images of destruction. "Broken promises," she sighed. "Broken dreams. Broken heart." She gazed at the nurse's face. She touched a finger to where her eye once was. "Broken face," she whispered. "Broken feet, breaking the bank. Break, broken." She bent to pick up the ravaged purple leather jacket. "Breaking to pieces," she said, as she held it in her arms like a child. She then began to rip the sleeves from it. "Break it in half," she grunted. "Broke, breaking, broke, break, broken."

The door opened. The plaid tweed suit and the red bowtie should have been a jarring sight themselves, but were overshadowed by the white, braided goatee that stretched from the man's chin to his navel.

He adjusted his Ben Franklin glasses on his aquiline nose and set his suitcase down.

The nurse did not greet him, but merely said. "I feel the time is right for a man of your talents."

"I would say so," came the soft Southern drawl, Louisiana, maybe.

The girl looked up at the man. "She broke it," she pleaded." She held up the shredded jacket to him like an offering. "It broke. It broke so easy. Break. Broken." She dropped it to her lap. "Why did it break?" she asked.

Mr. Price knelt beside her. "Strange and serene," he spoke to her. "Mythical and real." He took her hands in his. "Now I know your name."

"Why did you break it?" she said.

He stared deeper into her eyes. "Your identity is no longer a secret," he said, his voice calming. "I can look you in the eyes. I can spit in your face."

She grabbed the coat and pressed her face deep into it. "Broken," she cried, pounding her head. "It broke."

He took her hands and pressed them against his face, and he took his hands and pressed them against hers. Their stares locked into one another. He spoke. "Your power is dying," he said softly, assuring." Your hold is gone," he said. "For now, I hold the power, for now I know your name."

She began to tremble. "She broke my heart," she mumbled. "Break, broken. I broke her heart. Broken"

"I can hide if I want to," Mr. Price said. His lips were mere inches from hers. "Run if I want to. The choice is now mine."

"Broke the book," she said. "Broke the neck. Break, broken, broken breaking. It's broken." She looked deep into his eyes. "Why is it broken?" she asked him.

Mr. Price smiled. "The sins of a child or mind are now pardoned," he said. "If I want to pay, I will of my own accord, for now I know your name."

She pulled away from him, softly and timidly. "Broken heart," she said, clutching at her breast. "Broken hearts, broken heart, broken hearts." She fell to her knees and wept.

He stood, smiling. He glanced over to the one-eyed nurse and nodded.

The one-eyed nurse bent down and gathered up the remnants of the purple fur jacket.

The girl shrieked and flung herself towards the nurse. Mr. Price stepped forward between them. He caught the girl around the waist, and, spinning her around like a toddler, he dropped her to the ground. "Follow the lines until they lead to the end," he said. He raised his two fingers before her eyes. "Don't fight the trip," he said. "Fight the pain. Ride the rail, not the track." He crouched down before her and kneeled. "Peel back the covers and submit. Walk and talk and speak."

She shook her head back and forth. He held her gently." Shhh, Listen, fellow weeper," he said. "Don't fear the freefall. Hang on and see it through. Don't deny it. Roll with it, jive with it. It'll be over soon."

He lifted her head with a bent finger under her chin and looked into her eyes. There was an emptiness beginning there. He smiled, and asked, "Why?"

It took several moments before she spoke. "Dark," she said. "Warm…Safe."

He nodded and asked again. "Why?"

Her brow furrowed as she fumbled through the mist for the words. "Breathe in, breathe…. out. Each… breath… hanging… in the air, like… smoke from a fire… oh so long ago."

"It's the kind of breath that shows that you're alive," he said softly. "Or does it?"

She looked confused, but he continued. "Each breath is your soul. You give life to each hanging wisp. Those inhalations and exhalations, little by little, co-mingle in the atmosphere like lovers." He took her hands again. "Do it fast enough, he said, "and you will see stars."

She began to do so, breathing in and breathing out, inhaling and exhaling, faster and faster, until her eyes rolled back inside her head and she slumped.

He stood her up and held her. "The passage is open, step in if you dare," he soothed her. "Step into the mist, child. Don't fear the Machine, for it is often the birthplace of words. Remember, as the sun sets here, it rises in someone else's eastern sky. Unending, undying."

The one-eyed nurse smiled. This was not the first time she and Mr. Price had assisted someone into the fold. While she herself chose not to follow in the ways of her father and mother, she saw service to the Machine as a noble act, albeit time consuming. Mr. Price, however, was the best at what he did.

Mr. Price had a vice, and his memory had a secret.

He once had his own little room. It was a neatly kept room, well-lit and sterile. Several work stations ran along one wall, each with a telescopic magnified light and stool. In the middle of the room stood a large raised panel, covered with buttons and switches. It looked like a control panel straight out of a 1960's Mission Control station, right down to the teal sides and grey metallic hardware.

He had been a young man, then, and he wasn't Price. He was Nussbaum, working for the Man In Charge.

"Push that red button on the panel," The Man In Charge called out, still not looking up from his paperwork.

Nussbaum turned to the space-age control panel. In amongst the plethora of buttons and dials, one of the buttons was blinking a bright red. He reached out and pressed the button. The blinking stopped.

The Man In Charge looked up and stared straight ahead of him, off into space. "You pushed it, didn't you?"

"Yes," Nussbaum replied.

"You pushed it without question," The Man In Charge said, still not looking towards him. "You had no idea what that button was for, yet you pushed it anyway."

"You asked me to," Nussbaum, now second-guessing himself.

"What if I told you that the button you just pressed activated a complex flooding system, instantly filling a watertight room packed with innocent people with over 15 feet of water?"

Nussbaum could feel the colour drain from his face. "But why would you even have such a..."

The Man In Charge stood. "That is not the point! You did something simply because someone told you to. You did not stop to think why or to question why." He walked over to Mr. Price. "This is either a very important skill to possess," he placed his hand on the control panel. "or a terrible one."

Nussbaum tried to find clarification in his eyes. "So, which one is it?" he demanded. "Did I just kill a roomful of people? What does that button do?"

The Man In Charge smiled. "That button," he said, "blinks."

Mr. Price remembered the night it finally went for him. He inhaled deeply through his nose. The smells of the street, the filth and decay mingled with the smell of the rain. He found himself spinning clockwise, slowly at first, his arms flung out. He kept his eyes closed and his arms outstretched like Christ.

His speed increased, faster and faster, the soles of his leather shoes scraping like a needle at the end of a phonograph record. He spun for nearly twenty seconds, until he stopped perfectly still.

When he opened his eyes, He found himself facing the doors of a bar. He had been inside many times in the past.

"Is this where you want me?" He asked the voice in his head. It was as close to an answer as he could have expected for a long time, speaking to the darkness.

He stepped inside the doors. There were only a few derelicts in the room at that hour, their lost eyes gazing no further than the bottle before them.

He stepped up to the bar. A portly man with a handlebar moustache met him.

"What can I get you?" he asked in a raspy voice.

He opened my hand. In it was a twenty-dollar bill. "I want to know who the man is that is doing the killing."

He scoffed at this. "Ha! You and me both." He picked up an empty glass and began to clean it. "That bastard's killed five of my best customers." He looked the stranger over. "Are you a newspaper man?" he asked.

He shook his head. "I'm just a man looking for answers." He closed his fist over the money and turned from the bar.

The rain let up a bit, and he stepped off the curb and onto the street. He was beginning to feel hungry.

He turned and ran towards the scream. He passed one alleyway, then two, until he reached the point where the scream had come from. He ducked into the alleyway.

A figure knelt over a body lying facedown in the pavement.

He knelt and looked at the kneeling figure. "What happened?" He asked.

It was a little old woman. She wiped her eyes. "I don't know," she sobbed.

"What happened between when you left the bar and here?" The voice in his head spoke through him.

She looked at the man queerly. "The bar? I wasn't there." She replied.

"Don't be stupid, I just saw you leave with this man from there!" The voice in his head spoke through him again.

She began to shake her head. "I swear it weren't me, I swear." Her body began to shake and tremble before fainting dead away.

He took hold of the man's body and turned it over. His brown eyes were open, staring off into a space from which there is no return. His mouth was slightly open, and he could smell the gin upon his lips. The Man In Charge was in Charge no more.

He could hear a shuffling sound further down the alley. He gave chase.

The alley curved and turned into a dead end. He looked around and then straight up towards the rooftops.

"It's me!" he yelled out. "It's me! Wait!" There was only silence and the sounds of the city.

He sighed heavily. The voice in his head had told him that he would always be a step behind. He slammed his fists into the stone walls around him. "Shit, shit, shit, shit, shit!" He cried out. He looked down at his hands. The muck of the wall coated the heels. He rubbed them down the legs of his trousers and walked down the alleyway towards the body.

He rounded the corner to find himself in the midst of uniforms.

They shone their flashlights towards him. "Stop right there!" a voice shouted. Two of the uniforms ran up and took hold of his arms.

"Explain yourself!" one of the uniforms barked.

He opened his mouth to speak, but was interrupted by the little old woman. "No, it wasn't him, he came along after."

The Uniform looked at him. "Is this true?" he asked.

He nodded. "I heard the scream, and came running. I heard a shuffle down the alley, but found it to be a dead end."

The Uniform's eyes lowered into a squint. "A dead end, you say?" He looked at another uniform. "You might want to have a look."

The other uniform hurried down the alley, and then returned. "He's right," he stated, "just a dead end."

The man looked at the uniforms. "Please release my arms," The voice in his head said through him in an authoritarian tone.

They let him go.

The voice in his head made a show of brushing off his shoulders and arms and said, "You have my statement, and now I am leaving." He stepped over the body and made his way back to the street.

"Wait a moment," The Uniform called out.

He stopped and turned.

"We need your name," the Uniform said.

He smiled. "Price," the voice replied, "Mr. Price." He turned and walked back into the dying night.

Many years passed. Nussbaum was long gone. Mr. Price had controlled him for so long. Mr. Price would tell him what it wanted done, and he did what Mr. Price said. He knew the punishment if he didn't obey. The nights and days he spent in pain, wanting to claw his head apart to get to Mr. Price and rip it out of his brain, but to no avail. It was Mr. Price that made him hunt. It was Mr. Price that made him cut. He was only doing what Mr. Price commanded him to do.

The rubble of a massive building stood nearly 15 feet tall. The few standing bits of structure showed that at one time, it had been an apartment building. What windows still kept their shape stood gaping to the skies, empty mouths with missing teeth in an eternal scream.

A slab of unbroken brick stood upright upon the rubble. It was nearly twenty feet wide and eight feet high. There appeared to be something spray painted upon the slab, which he could not make out from where he stood. Curiosity got the better of the voice in his head, and he crossed the street to get a better look.

No Power. No Lines.

He climbed and stumbled over the broken remnants of the building, reaching out for the words, a light to guide his way, the voice said.

He laid his hands upon the bricks, knowing full well what the words meant, and that this was meant for no one but him. He laid his head down on the cool slab and closed his eyes.

No Power, it said. No Power, No Lines. Did this mean Mr. Price was losing its grip on him?

He was brought back to attention by the hollow pitter-patter of the rain as it fell upon his coat and upon the brickwork.

He smiled and bowed his head, not in reverence, but to simply keep the rain from his eyes.

"Excuse me sir," came a creaky voice. He looked up from where he sat. A little old lady stood looking up at him, her bonneted head cocked to one side in an inquisitive manner.

He smiled. "What can I do for you?" the voice asked her.

"Well, for starters, you can tell me what you're doing sitting on what used to be my house," she said curtly.

He smiled back at her. "It's quite simple, madam. I am the king of the castle." The voice said through him.

She looked appalled. "You're what?" she croaked.

He stood and raised his hands to the sky. "I'm the king of the castle." He began to sway and dance upon the rubble, Mr. Price singing the nursery tune through him at the top of his lungs. "I'm the king of the castle, and you're the dirty rascal!" He laughed maniacally as he sang, his hands outstretched like a child.

The old lady croaked her displeasure. "You're crazy, that's what you are!"

He looked down at her again. "Crazy?" the voice quizzed. He stopped dancing and made his way down the pile of bricks and rubble. "Crazy? Well then!"

He took hold of her hands and began to spin her around in circles, the whole time singing this nursery rhyme. She screamed and struggled, but her cries went unheard on the deserted street.

He dragged her to the top of the rubble pile. "Was this a nice house? Did you enjoy it?" the voice asked sarcastically. Grabbing a brick, he spun around and smashed her in the head with it.

She fell halfway down the rubble, nearly dead. He scurried down the pile and carried her body to the side of the pile that could not be seen from the street.

Descending the rubble pile, he straightened his clothing. Mr. Price was a clean and meticulous man. This brick dust would not do.

Mr. Price opened his eyes. The Girl opened hers.

CHAPTER 6

"Tell me about the girl," The Doctor finally asked me.

I sat in a much more comfortable chair now in his office. They had me back in the clothing I had run away from in the first place. "It was those eyes that caught me first," I said. "Jade inlaid with an ebony core. She was a shadow. The coming frost intercepted her."

The Doctor shook his head. "I'm not sure I follow," he said.

I laughed. "Her and her alone," I said, "All I wanted was a roll in the hay. Was that too much to ask?" I leaned forward and rested my hands upon his desk. "See, fall in love with me and it is forever. To hurt you is to hurt me too. When the anger rises within a beast like me, I can't seem to listen to the voices telling me, 'Let it go, man, she's a big girl. She can fight her own battles. If she needs a knight in shining armour, she'll ask." I leaned back. "There's a million shades of black out there, and a thousand shades of red. Make your mark and she will follow." I sipped from the cup in front of me. "I would hear myself say, 'but I don't want to do it. Why should I?' And someone would say, 'you must.'"

The Doctor wrote this down.

I peered over his desk and read his scribbles upside down. "You know," I said. "It's probably not safe to save these words."

"Don't worry, I'll be careful," he replied.

"That's what scares me," I said.

"Why does it scare you?" he asked.

"Because careful men make for a cowardly life," I said.

He leaned back in his chair. "You know," he said, "it's interesting that you feel uneasy about my documenting our conversations, Lieutenant." He put the pen down. "I assure you that this is a safe place. Anything you say here remains confidential. Any questions you have will be answered."

I sat up at this. "Really?" I asked with a chipper voice.

"Yes," the Doctor replied.

"Ok," I said, and leaned forward. "What would you say to me if I said that I was blind? What would my dead eyes see through the sands of time? What is there to be had when the son of god and the Son of Sam and a son of a bitch unite in a lunatic mind? Can one be impotent and still the father of man? Has antiquity caught up to us? Is the world now numb?" I leaned forward. "I have run away from your concrete and steel asylum. I have fled to the safety of open water, to the safety of frozen trees. Those trees have never lied, even as you killed them all. They never said a single dishonest word. All they did was inhale poison and expel life."

The Doctor's shoulders slumped. "I think that's all we'll have for today," he said, closing the file on his desk."

"Wait!" I said, "Where are the madmen? Where are the freaks they promised us? Sir, says I, I ask you this, has your consciousness ever been altered?"

He shook his head. "No, Lieutenant, it has never."

I sat back in my chair. "Then, my story I cannot tell. For unless your perception has been warped, all that I will say will be untrue."

He pressed a button on his desk. A buzzer sounded somewhere off in the distance. The Doctor stood.

"OK," I said, holding up my hands. I'll tell you this. I was in London. I sat there in a bar, the glass before me quickly running dry. The waitress had a nice ass, at least that's what the beer had told me…"

"Please," the Doctor held up his hand.

I ignored him and continued. "'I am a stranger from a strange land,' I mumbled to her softly, and I appreciated the friendly face. She smiled and asked me where I was staying. 'Nowhere,' I replied."

"We're finished, Lieutenant," he said.

I continued. "'Well,' she said, 'I have an extra bed at my place. You are welcome to it.'"

The guards entered and took me under the arms.

"I stayed there two days," I said as they took me out of the room. "I never did see that extra bed."

He stared down at the blood that covered his hands. He smiled and chuckled, his eyes glistening.

I did it, he thought to himself. I went through with it. I can't believe I had the balls to do it, but I've done it.

The phone on the wall broke the spell. He slipped his hand onto the receiver and brought the phone to his ear.

"Hello?" he said, trying his best to sound calm and collected.

"Where are you?" the female voice on the other end said sharply. "The meeting starts in 15 minutes!"

He looked down at his watch. It showed 8:45. The face was flecked with spots of blood.

He said nothing, and hung up.

He stood and looked around the room. It was everywhere, on the walls, on the ceiling, and on him.

He stepped out of the room and did not look back. Within minutes, the bloody clothes were in a dumpster and strolled naked and unseen.

The wheels were set in motion, he thought with a smile. It was the last step, the last quest, and now nothing they could do would stop what was coming. He walked forward into morning, assured in his work. The sky was clear, but the forecast called for flurries.

Mr. Price returned to the present moment from his daydream. He saw the girl in front of him. He lifted her hands. "Tell me," he said.

She smiled and held her head high, facing skyward. "My body became a battlefield," She orated. "The sickness created strange thoughts."

"And what shall we do to heal the sickness?" Mr. Price asked.

"Dig your toes into the earth, my brother," she said. "Like we did as children."

"Why children?" Mr. Price asked.

"We must look through a child's eyes, and be new again," she replied.

Mr. Price smiled. "What we create is immortal," he said. "They are but gods for us to worship. They cannot die, love or hate. They can only spark the soul." He placed his hands upon her shoulders. Remember that entropy is the greatest art," he said.

She nodded and sat down.

Mr. Price turned to the One-eyed nurse. "I think our work here is complete," he said.

"Your work," she replied, "not mine."

He smiled. "You're as culpable as I am. Remember; you called me."

"I called you in an attempt to find out how the girl acquired the cubes," said the one-eyed nurse. "The act of turning her into one of your cultish sisters of mercy was a side benefit solely for you."

Mr. Price Smiled. "And for that I am grateful. She will serve the cause wonderfully."

The one-eyed nurse lit a cigarette. "Mr. Price," she began. "What manner of choice does your order permit?"

"I beg your pardon?" he asked.

"Shouldn't your heart be yours to give?" She asked.

"Only to those who serve their betters," he said.

The one-eyed nurse smiled. "Mr. Price, I've observed you over the past few weeks, and I think I've absorbed enough of your mumbo-jumbo to bullshit my way through this fractured system we live in."

"Oh, but surely," Mr. Price began.

"Let me finish," The one-eyed nurse said. "In spite of your proselytizing, I learned long ago that, in order to survive, you never let those who want power and devotion guide your tastes again. For then they have you by the balls. You shouldn't have to steal bits of tomorrow to survive today."

She opened the door. "Mr. Price, as you have failed to ascertain the specific details as to how this patient managed to be in possession of some 6 dozen cubes of classified materiel while in the company of an Army officer who abandoned those soldiers under his command during battle and subsequently fled their massacre and went A.W.O.L., I am sorry to say that your services will no longer be required at this institution. Good day to you."

Mr. Price's face hardened, and he spoke. "The matter of the patient…"

"The matter of the patient is of no longer concern to you. Now, I'm sure you quite know the way out."

Without a word, he walked out the door.

The one-eyed nurse closed the door and turned to face the girl. "Poor child," she said. She walked over to the girl and placed her hands upon her head. “May your choices be your own. May they be good decisions, made of their own accord. The sins of us all have paid for their freedom.”

CHAPTER 7

I stood in the dock before those gathered to judge me. I cleared my throat and began to speak. "I am an honest man. I have two honest hands, and things as I understand them will never go away. With my honest hands, I've tried to help my fellow man. I always thought you did the same. But what I have seen has led me to believe that you've been playing with the people like pieces in a game.

"A game. It's all a game, where you change the rules, and where we look the fools so you can buy yourself some glory upon the backs of those who have come to you. They come to you with their demons screaming in their ears, their young lives lived in mortal fear. They aren't sure if they'll live the year. They are soldiers coming back from war; these fellow men from whom you tore the faith they had in life itself. I watched you hang an innocent man after stabbing him in the back." I glared into the eyes of the man who had once been my brother-in-arms, a man upon whom I had marched into the darkness alongside so often, and who had betrayed so many of us to the Machine. "No more can this honest man commit to you his honest hands for service to your crooked plans. Seek another pawn. My time with you is done."

The Mad Judge smiled, then looked over his shoulder to the man dressed in black leather who would be my murderer. "The Lieutenant is hereby found guilty of desertion and dereliction of duty resulting in death of those in his command. The sentence is death, following the standard interrogation." He banged his gavel. "Major, Dig the holes where the posts go in. Drop them in and pack them tight. Nail the wire to the fence. That should keep them in."

I put my head back on the stone wall and thought about my misery. My body trembled from the denial, the prohibition of my trade. I smiled and thought about that night, and that offer of a helping hand. I spat blood on the floor. The chute slid open, and a bucket of water dropped in. "Your kindness is like a kiss of death," I yelled. "It's an invitation to dig my own grave, with you providing me with a spade. I'd rather you be rude to me!" I threw my head back and sang as off key as I could muster.

"Oh, mercy me,
There's a threat to be seen
By soldiers and saints
In a cruel twist of fate
Read into her mind
To a time so sublime
Where once there held sway
All the times that we said that
We'd always be free and
We'd never retreat from
That which we believe to be
The truth we hold deep
And we swore that we'd never
Sleep."

My head dropped. My avarice had been denied. I was like the snake I used to keep in a glass case; irrationally feared by what others of my kind are capable of doing, but unable to follow through because of the glass.

Perhaps we'd both realized that what we see is merely an illusion, merely the reflection of the inside of the cage hiding the visions of the outside, with this invisible and limiting wall of reality in between. I could see freedom there before me, but upon approach, I met a cold an unmovable barrier. "You cannot believe that this is my end!" I called out to my keepers. "Mine is a spirit that cannot be contained by mere chains!"

Who was I kidding? A prison is a prison, whether it is a gilded cage or stone and barbed wire. Each of us is our own warden. We are all guilty of it. We are the bullies. We are the maniacs. We are the drunks that get behind the wheel of our own destinies. The minute we took the Oath, we defaulted our worth to the Machine, the massive God-damn Machine, where we seek our solace and lose our humanity. We are, all of us, addicts to the core.

My crime was that I had a brain, and a strong brain. I looked up into the rafters and saw the puppeteer above us all and dared asked him his name. I questioned, and for this unholy utterance, my conditional freedom was forfeit. I was not a leader of men. I could barely lead myself. I did not kill those boys. The enemy slaughtered them. Many would have died had I been there. Was there blood upon my hands? Was THEIR blood upon my hands? Either way, young men were going to die. I simply chose not to be one of them.

The keys rattled as the guard opened the door. "It's time," he said.

She stepped in and touched my head. "Please stand," she said.

I did no such thing. "You're going to break my heart again," I said. There's nothing I can do to stop the coming of the pain."

She smiled and began to speak, but I stopped her. "So much lost, and very little gained. There's nothing left to say to you. I've been living in the wilderness, away from the 'he and she', with streams of consciousness swiftly flowing o'er me." I finally stood. "What you get is what you see. No longer will you see me going through the winds of change, or denying my partiality."

She turned to leave, but I stepped in front of her, my face in front of hers. I was not about to let her go without a fight. "You have no concept, do you? On which my very life's a stage, outgoing and incoming, not knowing and confounding? My sadness leaves a stain on those who dare to see what is going on with me. All those pretty things that I will not clean."

She bowed her head to avert my eyes. There was little left of the girl I knew. She was now a canvas someone else had painted on. Even the blonde hair had been replaced with the dark raven curls of her natural state.

She began to speak. "Why do you speak like Hamlet? Are you so insane that you don't even care to plead for your life when you're marked to die tomorrow? You're condemned, yet you speak in lyrics and meters." She lifted her head. "You know what to do," she said, her voice cracking.

"You once spoke this way with me, now you say that I already know the answers?" I hissed. "If that's the case, then what's with the delay? If my brain's prolonging my destruction, then why can't I steer the other way?"

"Perhaps the answer lies in perfection?" she offered.

"Perhaps it lies in living wicked sin," I countered. "Or perhaps it comes with Self-induced ignorance. I've done this all before. Yet it's still within; no answers, no insurance, no hope for future in here." I raised her face with one finger. "I fell in love with the raw humanity I thought I could see. It made me a fool, and I was locked in a room with no windows and a chalk outline on the floor."

"If you admit to your sins…" she said.

"Admit? Nothing can stop the screams of the dying portents and of all those things I've failed to be."

"What about the faith?" she asked.

I laughed loudly. "Faith? All that I need is some old-time religion, is that it? Give me a fire, a change of the season?" I circled her like she was Ophelia. "Chanting and twirling, around and around, bare feet upon the smooth surface of ground well-worn from the people who walked there before me? Faith, you say. Giving us only part of the stories well told by the wise ones, but slaughtered by Jesus, calling us evil and bastardized heathens? Burned in a fire fed by the male clergy convinced of their god's conditional mercy?"

She covered her ears with her hands and closed her eyes to shut me out.

I smiled. "Too close to the veil has my spirit journeyed, as harsh as the death of the summers hurts me."

The tears ran down her cheeks. I leaned in closer. "The prairie wind blows cold. It waters my eyes, too." I lightly tapped her on the forehead. "It's here, but it will vanish. My smile will turn to stone when this cloud of darkness covers me. It will cast a shadow 10 miles wide, and any spark of genius will run away." I kissed her lips. "This godforsaken misery has made me hard to take. Old friends fall to the wayside and new ones are hard to make. I loved you once, and thought that perhaps you had felt the same. It's hard to capture feelings when the spirit wants to die. The ink won't stop drying up, my pens keep dying. Greatness is expected, but all I can offer is simplistic rhyme. I'm not a little soldier boy anymore."

She closed her eyes and called for the guard. She stepped away without a word.

"They say we all have a twin somewhere," I called. "That same old face from the mirror we stare. I swore that I met yours today."

She turned, and I continued. "I thought I knew her far too well. I spat in her face and condemned her to hell." As she walked down the corridor, I called out to her. "Hey," I said.

She stopped, but did not turn.

"Where's your purple fur jacket?" I asked her.

She said nothing, but I saw her shivering under her robes. Quickly, she scurried down the corridor.

"Try as you may," the Major spoke, "there's no way you can outrun the Machine."

The victims pulled and strained at their restraints. They were cold and unaware.

I could almost read their thoughts as I sat tied to the racks. Why were they there? Had they not done what was asked of them? Hadn't they served the Machine faithfully?

The Major smirked as he ordered the restraints pulled tighter. "You see," he roared, "this Glorious Machine sees all and knows all, watches all and feels all. It can weed out the weak and reward the faithful." He flipped a switch, and a body vanished into a cloud of smoke and ashes.

The Major paused to wipe his hands on a towel. "The Machine demands the best. Its patience is razor thin." He turned to face me. This had been a display for me; this spilling of innocent blood. "Any final thoughts?"

I smiled. "The statues continue to fall, and the narrowminded lament over the passing of their ignorant history. I am paradoxical for no reason. It is far too easy for me to see how all the liars have conspired to put fear into the minds, so that they can drive you out into traffic in the middle of the night. I never bought into your reindeer games. I will not shave my head to please you."

The Major's face reddened, but I continued. "Yes, I stood and watched you dance your fancy dance for those from whom you want so much. If they knew the length of your misguided life design, they might want to make an issue."

I was slapped, but I continued. "It comes to me as no surprise, because heaven knows you tried to take and make and stake and break me. Well, sometimes it doesn't go that way, and you cannot make me stay to take more than I want, my dear Brutus." I paused. "Or is it Judas?"

"You bastard!" the Major screamed, his stoicism completely destroyed. He kicked me, but I continued. "I see the appeal of it all, for if our places were switched, the only time that I would feel alive is when your hands are bound and tied, the rope pulled tight against your skin, awakened feelings I cannot begin to explain. Never dreaming my freedom could come from your restraint, crucified just like a saint."

The Major's rage knew no bounds. He hit me with a cudgel, breaking open my lips. Still I continued. "Inhibitions cast aside; blindfolded eyes opened wide. I hold my breath as I pull your hair down hard towards me. Would you close your eyes, or keep them open to see if I am pleased?"

He grabbed me by the hair and brought his lips to mine. When he pulled away from the kiss, he wore my blood like a clown. His eyes said so much, yet he did not speak. The restraints were cut, and I was taken away.

The cell doors slammed. I was alone again. Through the floor, I could feel the vibration of the Machine, as another happy customer met their fate.

I was far too sublime to ease my own mind. My body was shaking. The wind blew. I was faking. The waves were breaking on the shore, and the notebooks and ledgers were now soaked to the core. My words were carried out to sea. I cannot swim, so there they'll be. Perhaps the wind will hear my songs; hers the only eyes to see what I have to say from this place where Pity drips from every pregnant pause. I was here, still wishing my poetry was pretty.

I awoke to the smell of smoke. The smell of smoke still triggered me; the sight of flames made me shiver. There would be no sleep for me tonight. The nightmares would take over, I could guarantee it.

Burning bits of paper rained down from above. The burning bits set my darkness alight. Those tiny glowing pinpricks of light, dying before they reached the floor of my oubliette.

It wasn't until one set fire to the rags that were my bed that I realized what it was that they were burning.

"Your sacrilege will not break my mind!" I cried to the darkness above. "I know that these are my books you are burning! The Captain shall hear of this!"

The thump of the severed head upon the floor brought me to my knees. I trembled as I picked it up.

"Captain, my captain," I whispered into his dead ears, "please forgive your forgotten son." I closed those dead decaying eyes and pushed the stray hairs from the grey face. "Yours was a death I feared more than my own." I laid the head down, and with trembling lips, I sang.

"At Queenston Heights and Lundy's Lane,
Our brave fathers, side by side,
For freedom, homes and loved ones dear,
Firmly stood and nobly died;
And those dear rights which they maintained,
We swear to yield them never!
Our watchword evermore shall be…"

I could sing no more. My fight faltered; my soul scarred. I had followed this man through the mud and the gas. We had fought through the barbed wire; out of sight from the eyes of the Machine, swearing oaths to each other that we would bring the fight to the Machine when we could arise from our watery graves and turn for home.

Home. It was a concept that mattered little to me now. Those black streets, empty and deadly. I once heard someone say that the shadows were your best friends on the streets. A shadow could hide anything, or anybody. The shadows were your guardian angels who watched over every night as the sun died and the stars came out. The shadows could hide your guilt, and as long as you lived by the cover of night, what happened in the shadows would stay there, never to see the light of day. Once, I was ashamed of where I came from. Now, I wanted to wear it like a Badge of Honour. As the snake sheds its skin, so must the mind. Leave the stupidity of youth once you have outgrown it.

I picked up the Captain's head. "The Fascists have stormed the Citadel. The Good and True people are now the Resistance. They are behind the lines of the Enemy. We saw the Enemy from the Eastern Watch Tower as they approached through the morning mist, Captain. Their numbers were not as great as first imagined, sir, and we thank god for that. Once upon a time, we walked those cobblestones," I spoke to those dead ears. "We watched the rain fall down around us, so very far from this home we imagined, with those Roman ruins beneath our feet." I laid the head down reverently once again. "But that was so very long ago. Short by Greenwich Mean Time, but a lifetime away from me, now. King and Empire have fallen to the Machine, and progress waits for no men, does it, my Captain? Forward movement is supposed to feel good. The sun shall never set on my memories." I laid the head down upon the floor. "It's been years, but I can still feel the slice of the blade.

♦ ♦ ♦

They awoke me at dawn. They mumbled and screamed in their clicking voices. I turned away and was struck for my troubles. I turned back around and smiled sweetly. "I've forgotten the question. Could you ask me again? I wasn't paying attention. What was that you said?"

Her soft hand upon my cheek soothed me but for a moment. "You mustn't fight, love," she began.

I bit her hand so hard that I could taste her blood. "I've not declared war upon the kingdom of love," I growled.

She took back her hand, and for my effort, I was struck. "If biting you is all it takes to be beaten to death, then by all means, sit by my side so that I may eat you." I laughed.

The Major stepped forward. "On your feet, you degenerate, confederate excuse. The Machine awaits."

As I made no effort, they made it for me. "I thank you for having shorn my locks, fat Shepherd. It has given you less to manhandle me by."

It was his turn to smile. He leaned in close and sneered into my face. "I'm only sorry that you have been rendered with no ears and no balls to grab hold of."

I counted the steps between my cell and the Machine. Two hundred and six, and seven, and eight, and nine.

The belts were secured tightly around me. My chest was made bare, and the electric leeches applied, seven to my left breast and nine to my right. The wires began to burn my skin as the Machine whirred.

"Now is your last chance to confess," The Major said. He looked down at me. "Will you take this one last chance?"

Through the one eye they left in me, I returned his gaze. "One last kiss before I go?" I said weakly.

She stepped forward. "Did you ask them?" I asked her.

"Yes, I did."

"What did they say?"

"They gave no reply."

I smiled. "See? Was that so hard? All you had to do was tell a little white lie. It's so much cheaper than selling your soul." I asked for a kiss. She gave me one. "The end is the beginning of thee. The beginning is the end of the beginning. Beginning the…the…the…Goddamnit, I've lost my train of thought."

I looked to the Major. "Now, can I please ask you my question?"

The Major replied, "you may proceed."

I smiled a very weak smile. "Oh, good! Now Major, what I want to know is this: what do you know about the 15th Century Kings of England?"

"I know nothing of the subject," He replied.

My smile widened. "No? Oh, excellent! I mean, not 'excellent' in the fact that you are unaware, but what I mean is that I, as an educator have the opportunity to teach you." I wiggled a little to get comfortable. "You see, Edward IV was King of England, the first Yorkist king of England, in fact, who reigned twice. The first reign was from 1461 to 1470, then again for a second time, from 1471 to his death in 1483."

The Major was unfazed. "What does any of this have to do with sentence?"

I chuckled. "History is immensely interesting, Major. We need to learn from it. The king of whom I speak reigned during a time known as the Wars of the Roses. Have you ever heard of it?"

The Major said nothing, so I continued. "I don't blame you for not knowing, really. It was an awfully long time ago, and it was a very brutal and violent time."

My death held no pain. A moment's discomfort, but it passed. The multitude of lights and colours that danced before me were not as grand as I had expected. It was as if a child had thrown pastel pieces of paper into the air. I began to count back each step. Two hundred and nine, and eight, and seven, and six. I counted back to one, and it left me.

I still think of her, although I am locked forever in this state between there and here. I can still see her in her purple fur jacket, I wonder if she still bears that tattoo of the raven's claw upon her breast, or did she make it an offering to the Machine? Did the choir sing as she sliced into her skin, and did she fanatically smile as she dropped the bleeding flesh into the gaping maw of the Machine? She smiled as such when they fed my manhood and my ears to it. She grinned, and she wiped my blood on her arms. She grinned.

So, I float here, and I wonder, and I dream, and if I still had my honest hands, I would write. Lord almighty, would I write.

EPILOGUE

The Scene: a shrouded object sits stage right, and a podium centre stage. Light organ music plays. Figure walks in, wearing loud 1970's tweed suit. Figure uncovers shrouded object, revealing it to be a coffin upon a set of sawhorses. He lifts the lid, revealing it to be empty.

"Dearly beloved, we are gathered here tonight to pay our last and final respects to a much loved, respected and influential friend in our lives. I would like to take a few moments, if I may, to say a few words to commemorate and, dare I say, celebrate, the life and achievements of our good friend who lies here before us.

"We all know that this soul had a troubled life here on earth, as have we all from time to time, but now, brothers and sisters, the journey has ended for our dear departed friend, the Muse.

The Muse was born so very long ago, far from here, in a cold and dark place, where light was a stranger. So, one might say, the muse came straight from where the sun doesn't shine, which makes a lot sense, for who among us of the creative persuasion has never wished that they could simply pull a creative idea out of their ass?

"This Muse was also a pain in that ass, putting in our minds the image of what we wish to create, and when the finished product looks not quite like what we had in our minds, we would curse and blaspheme the Muse, and question our own artistic talents and merits.

"Let us also not forget that this was an asshole who would call you in the middle of the night, waking you from your sleep with 'hey, I got an idea, and it needs to be worked on right NOW, because it'll be gone by sunrise. Who cares if it's 3 AM and you have to work in the morning?' Oh, the Muse was a going concern, causing havoc and consternation wherever it travelled.

"I would be remiss if I didn't mention the odd sense of humour that the Muse possessed. How it would say to one artist, 'I want you to take your brushes and pigments and paint the massive ceiling of the Sistine Chapel in the glory of the Almighty' and then, turning to another artist and say, 'I want you to paint one red stripe across a blank canvas, then, climb into a bathtub filled with human excrement, say 'there is no god' and call it 'avant-garde performance art.'

"The Muse we are laying to rest today was born of an 8-year-old child, viewing a parent in a box very similar to this one. That 8-year-old child went on to see grandparents, uncles and aunties, cousins and friends, well-known and barely known people in the child's life, heavily made up and cold to the touch, placed into the ground in one of these boxes.

"You see, these receptacles of corporeal remains are what was known as 'Indian Affairs Coffins', because this is, for all intents and purposes, the most...economical casket that could be provided. Why, a closer inspection would reveal that this box, simple and dignified as it is, is really constructed of the same type of sawdust and glue particleboard that makes up every rickety bookcase and entertainment centre sold by your local department store. If you're a braver soul, why, you might look a little deeper, and see that the body lies upon shredded office paper and fliers, over which is the same type of paper that lines the examination table in your doctor's office.

"It is a box, a wooden box. Nothing really all that frightening or scary about a wooden box, is there? Why, this is a wooden box. It once held cigars. This too is a wooden box. It held iced tea. You know, the really shitty iced tea that you're supposed to leave out in the sun?

"Funny, If I were to offer you this box and say, 'here, take this home and put something in it,' you might take it with a smile, say 'thank you' and put buttons or spare change in it. I doubt you'd go home and put iced tea in it, even though it was built to hold iced tea. Same thing with the cigar box. I seriously doubt that this box would ever hold a cigar in it again.

"Now, what if I said to you, 'I want you to take this box here, this beautifully lined and ornamented box, I want you to take it home', I doubt you would. Sure, one or two of you might, those of you out there who like to dress in black. You might say, 'Sure! It'll go really good with the one we already got in the bedroom!' And, I will admit to being curious as to seeing what you would put in it, if you catch my drift.

"But most of the people here would say no. Not because it's big and weighs a significant amount and takes up quite a bit of space. You would say no because it's a casket, a coffin, a thing to put dead people in. Even though there has never been a body inside this box. Even though it is clean and empty, just the thought of what it is would make you say no.

That seed was planted in that young child's mind at the age of 8. That was part of the Muse's sense of humour that I told you about: instill in a young mind an irrational fear of an inanimate object.

"The Muse grew with that 8-year-old. As childhood pet goldfish were buried with full regimental funerals to the strain of 'TAPS', and as visits to graveyards became a treasured pastime.

"It wasn't the dead that attracted the Muse, no no no. It was the accoutrements that go along with it: The beauty of a wonderfully crafted and highly polished mahogany box, much different and more expensive than this one. It was the sleek lines and smooth movement of a hearse coming around the corner with the sun glinting off the chrome landau bars. It was the magical incantations of a holy man guiding the deceased across the River Styx, and finally, it was beautifully carved granite or marble stone that proclaimed 'HERE LIES" or 'IN LOVING MEMORY OF'.

"What the Muse loved, more than anything, was that its appreciation of such things made it different from you, and that these things made you…uncomfortable…uneasy…dare I say, frightened.

"I would like you all for a moment to pause and reflect upon what you are feeling at this moment. Now, compare that with how you felt the moment that you saw this box. I imagine that there are many of you here tonight who, in spite of how much I proselytize upon the subject, are still feeling very out-of-sorts just being in the same room with this here box. I'm betting that the 'Heebee Jeebies' are sitting upon your shoulders. You know, that is an awful lot of power to give to an object, especially one that's designed to only do one thing. It not like a painting or a sculpture. Those are meant to make you feel something.

"This is a container, like your coffee cups or your desk drawers or your handbags. It is only meant to contain something. This box isn't going to hurt you, unless it falls on you. By the time any of us get to this box, whatever was going to hurt you has already done its job.

"For a lot of us here, the feelings and emotions that arise from this all come not from the box, but from those people for whom the last time we saw them in any shape or form in this life was inside one of these. That's alright. We mourn those we have lost.

"Tonight, dear friends, we mourn another loss: something that once drove the machinery of creativity. We mourn the loss of inspiration, of expression, of design and ideas. We are marking the passage of a trailblazer, who has finally come to the end of its trail.

The Muse was a friend and an enemy, a lover and opponent. The Muse rode shotgun and the Muse drove the getaway car. It was our partner in crime, and it was a witness for the Prosecution. It was there when we needed it the most, and it was often nowhere to be found.

"Now, brothers and sisters, we are all united in our common quest to see the world in a much better light than it actually is. Many of us have joined hands and joined the struggle for a better world, indeed, I've heard people quote the phrase 'I want to leave the world a better place than we ourselves had." As much as the Muse would have loved to have taken credit for that, I'm afraid that our dearly departed friend before us could never have created that feeling.

"The Muse was but a mirror, reflecting back at us our own feelings and emotions. For each of us, it was a different mirror. Some of those mirrors were broken, some were funhouse mirrors that distorted and warped what we saw reflected. Some were filthy mirrors that needed a good spray of glass cleaner. The most honest mirrors, however, were not mirrors at all. They were simply panes of glass-windows keeping some people out, while at the same time, keeping other people in, but all the time letting everybody see everybody else. Those mirrors, my friends, are the rarest of all.

"It is fitting to know that, while we are gathered here tonight in this bucolic setting with good food and fellowship, lamenting our late friend, a glimpse into this box would show it to be empty. You see, the bastard didn't even show up for its own funeral. The Muse is out there somewhere tonight, running amok. I can only imagine what the bugger will come up with next."

ALSO AVAILABLE

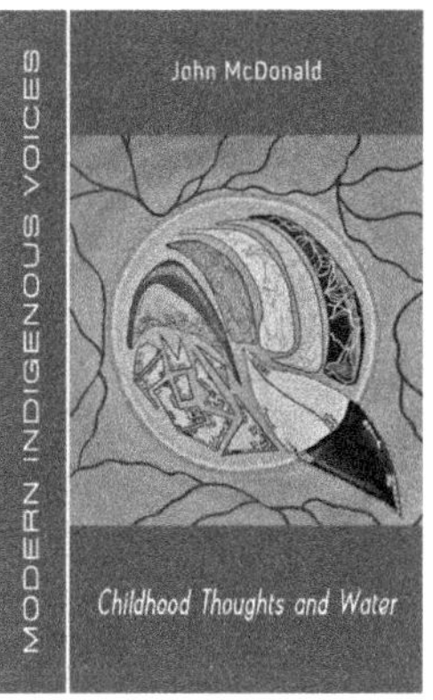

Childhood Thoughts and Water is a collection of Beat Poetry, Spoken Word, Performance Art and Lyrical Verse. This is a work that journeys into the memories and events of an Urban Indigenous warrior's struggles to reconnect with a language and culture that are seemingly always almost out of his reach. The common theme of reconnecting with nature and with water is interspersed with the imagery of childhood recollections and anecdotes about life and love, aspirations and defeats, and the desire to achieve greatness in spite of the obstacles and barriers inherent in a life lived on the fringes, in the shadows and on the streets, in the spotlight and behind the backstage curtain.

www.ingramcontent.com/pod-product-compliance
Ingram Content Group UK Ltd.
Pitfield, Milton Keynes, MK11 3LW, UK
UKHW062308290726
14090UKWH00018B/947

9 781772 311495